Rudow's Guide to Modern Jigging

By Lenny Rudow

Published by Schiffer Publishing Ltd.
Rudow's Guide to Modern Jigging was originally published
by Geared Up Publications, LLC. in 2009.
Copyright © Geared Up Publications, LLC. 2009
Reprint Copyright © 2012 Lenny Rudow

Library of Congress Control Number:2012938142

All rights reserved. No part of this work may be reproduced or used in any form or by any means—graphic, electronic, or mechanical, including photocopying or information storage and retrieval systems—without written permission from the publisher.
The scanning, uploading and distribution of this book or any part thereof via the Internet or via any other means without the permission of the publisher is illegal and punishable by law. Please purchase only authorized editions and do not participate in or encourage the electronic piracy of copyrighted materials.
"Schiffer," "Schiffer Publishing Ltd. & Design," and the "Design of pen and inkwell" are registered trademarks of Schiffer Publishing Ltd.

ISBN: 978-0-9787278-7-1
Printed in the United States of America

Schiffer Books are available at special discounts for bulk purchases for sales promotions or premiums. Special editions, including personalized covers, corporate imprints, and excerpts can be created in large quantities for special needs. For more information contact the publisher:

Published by Schiffer Publishing Ltd.
4880 Lower Valley Road
Atglen, PA 19310
Phone: (610) 593-1777; Fax: (610) 593-2002
E-mail: Info@schifferbooks.com

For the largest selection of fine reference books on this and related subjects, please visit our website at **www.schifferbooks.com**
We are always looking for people to write books on new and related subjects. If you have an idea for a book, please contact us at proposals@schifferbooks.com

This book may be purchased from the publisher.
Please try your bookstore first.
You may write for a free catalog.

In Europe, Schiffer books are distributed by
Bushwood Books
6 Marksbury Ave.
Kew Gardens
Surrey TW9 4JF England
Phone: 44 (0) 20 8392 8585; Fax: 44 (0) 20 8392 9876
E-mail: info@bushwoodbooks.co.uk
Website: www.bushwoodbooks.co.uk

Dedication:

This book is dedicated to all of my fishing buddies, who make time spent on the water a good time regardless of the catch. The list is too long to spell out, but you know who you are!

Table of Contents

Introduction — p. 7

Part I: Techniques & Equipment

Chapter 1: Tried and True – Traditional Vertical Jigging — p. 15

Chapter 2: The Motion of the Ocean – Speed Jigging — p. 29

Chapter 3: Meet the Jiggers – Meat Jigging — p. 43

Chapter 4: No Child's Play – Yo-yoing — p. 53

Chapter 5: Jigging Gear – Rods and Reels — p. 61

Chapter 6: Jigging Tackle & Rigging – Lines, Leaders, and Jigs — p. 83

Chapter 7: Behind the Scenes - The Butterfly "System" — p. 113

Part II: Species-specific Jigging

Chapter 8: Big Game:
Tunas, Wahoo, and Mahi-mahi — p. 121

Chapter 9: Deepwater Dwellers:
Golden Tilefish, Wreckfish, and Grouper — p. 133

Chapter 10: Other Bottom Fish:
Blueline Tilefish, Rosies, and Shark — p. 143

Chapter 11: The Wrecking Crew:
Sea Bass, Snappers, and Grouper — p. 151

Chapter 12: Inshore Gamefish:
Stripers, Blues, Amberjack, Fluke, and Weakfish — p. 161

Introduction

Jigging has been around for eons, yet it's also what's hot and new these days. How can it be both at the same time? Because the term "jigging" has expanded to include many different varieties of fishing techniques. In fact, today there's vertical jigging, speed jigging, yo-yoing, meat-jigging and any number of combinations of these tactics. Add to this the fact that very recent advances in fishing gear have made it possible to tweak jigging styles as never before, and that these new presentations happen to be deadly-effective on several species of gamefish, and you have a craze on your hands. Oh, yes, and a massive marketing push from the likes of Shimano (the Butterfly system) doesn't hurt, either.

So, why jig? First and foremost, because you will encounter many situations where jigging will be the most effective way to

The author bends his jigging rod on a wreckfish, at Norfolk Canyon.

catch fish. In some places at some times, it'll be virtually the only way to get them to bite. And again, thanks to those modern advances in tackle manufacturing, jigging also allows you to present lures without additional rigging and weights, while using gear that's extremely light and comfortable compared to the size of the fish you're targeting. A 150-pound bluefin hooked on a rod that looks like striper gear? Landing that fish is completely realistic — and a hell of a lot of fun.

How did we get here? When the Butterfly system came onto the market, my BS alarm started ringing. My gut response was that Shimano did some great marketing and somehow, they had even managed to make jigging seem like a 'new' tactic. But they jigs weren't anything particularly special, and their cost was high. Then, on a boat-testing gig in Port Aransas, Texas, for *Texas Fish & Game* magazine, I ended up on a boat with Jeremy Sweet, a product specialist in the fishing tackle division at Shimano. While casting soft plastics for reds and specs on a backwater flat (a situation in which jigging is, of course, completely inapplicable,) the Butterfly system came up in conversation. In as polite a way as possible, I gave him my initial assessment. He gave me a dead-pan look for moment, then said "You're wrong. Try using the entire system — rods, reels, lines, jigs, and technique — and you'll change your mind. The Butterfly system really kicks ass in a lot of conditions that other techniques just won't work for." I bit my tongue and thought "yeah, right…"

Back at home a few weeks later, I put the ball in Shimano's court. I sent off a few e-mails challenging them to send someone out to Maryland, to show me the real speed-jigging deal. At the time I was

Shimano Rep Justin Poe, demonstrating the Butterfly system.

running a 28' McKee Craft with twin Yamaha F250's out of Ocean City, and I offered to take any Shimano rep out for two solid days of bluefin tuna fishing. Within a week Shimano got back to me with solid dates, and a commitment to send Justin Poe, all the way from their Irvine (California) facility, to break me in to Butterflying.

As often happens when it comes to fishing, our plans were ruined by the fish. Anyone who went offshore from a Delmarva port during late August of 2007 will probably remember that the tuna were MIA. Not just hard to find, but completely absent. As any good angler would, we adapted to the conditions and changed our game plan. These jigs were killers on wreck fish, Justin assured me, so sea bass should love 'em. And he was right. With four guys on the boat we had one fishing a bait rig as three others jigged, and the jigs out-fished the bait by at least two to one. That's not to say that the fish were twice as likely to eat metal over meat, but thanks to the top-rigged hooks used with Butterfly jigs, we jiggers rarely snagged the wreck. In fact, with three lines going full-tilt all morning we only lost five jigs. The bait user, meanwhile, was constantly getting snagged, broken off, re-rigging, and re-baiting. Just the one line lost five rigs in the same amount of time, proving it had triple the hassle-factor. Oh yes, and it also was catching a heck of a lot more small throw-backs then the jigs.

Wreck fishing proved the techniques' effectiveness, but it wasn't exactly what you'd call mind-blowing. That would come later in the afternoon, when we pushed offshore to try and locate golden tilefish. These fish live at the edge of the Continental shelf, and our hotspot was 750' deep. This time we switched the bait-versus-jig ratio, dropping down three baited lines while only Justin dropped a jig. Hey — we wanted to get some real meat into the boat, and what were the chances of catching a fish 750' down on a jig? Yet somehow, in the darkness far below the boat, a golden tilefish saw and attacked the Butterfly. It hit with an unmistakable smash — I could see it in the rod tip from 10' away — and fought hard for nearly 20 minutes. When it broke the surface a round of gasps went through the cockpit; it was a true monster golden. Back at the Ocean City Fishing Center, swinging from the scales it proved to be a mere six pounds shy of the IGFA world-record golden tilefish. At that point, I was convinced: there really was something to this Butterfly thing.

When the summer of 2008 rolled around, it looked like the tunas would be a bust again. Some guys were picking up one or two a day by trolling planer lines, but the fish were few and far between, so targeting them on the jig would be impossible. Still, when I ran offshore I brought the jigging gear just in case. And as we trolled around

Just six pounds shy of the world record, this is believed to be the first golden tilefish ever caught on a bare Butterfly jig.

not catching fish, I started to see a pattern: patches of bait kept popping up near the bottom at the south-east corner of the Ham Bone, a lump where the bottom dropped from 120' to 140'. Then, while passing over one exceptionally large patch of bait, I saw two hard red arches at 70' just below the thermocline. Tunas, no doubt. We rolled up the trolling gear, stowed it below-decks, and broke out the jigging sticks. Passing back over the spot we spotted the fish again, and sent those Butterflies dropping down through the depths. Within five minutes we were hooked up, and in the next five hours we experienced over a dozen bone-shaking, drag-ripping strikes. The biggest fish of the day was about 125-pounds, and it was caught on a rod that looks like it was built for casting lures to striped bass.

A very small rod, with a very big tuna on the end of the line.

That was the last day I set out a trolling spread on my boat for the rest of the year — but my crews and I tied into heavy-duty bluefin virtually every trip, for the rest of the season. That fall, jigs proved a hot ticket for stripers in the Chesapeake. Over the winter, it was again jigs that did the trick while going for wreckfish and blueline tilefish, off the Virginia coast. The next spring we out-fished our buddy boat (which was trolling with the traditional methods) while jigging for king mackerel in North Carolina. And as I sit here working on this book the rods and reels sitting behind me are still damp from yesterday, when fishing buddy Hank's jig was smashed by the first bluefin of the season. Now, I can't think of any form of fishing I'd rather apply. And once you use the techniques described in this book,

I'll bet you'll feel the same way about jigging. So as my very close personal fishing buddy Max says, "let's get jiggly with it."

Max got jiggly with it!

Part I: Techniques & Equipment

Chapter 1: Tried and True – Traditional Vertical Jigging

When I said jigging has been around for eons, I was talking mostly about traditional vertical jigging. I realize that 90 percent of the guys who read this book already know how to jig in this fashion, but I'm still going to cover the technique for two very specific reasons: First, I've been with a lot of really good jiggers who made mistakes — and have also learned from them that I'd been making plenty of mistakes of my own. No matter how good or experienced an angler you are, there's always more to learn. So hopefully, even experienced jiggers will pick up a tidbit or two in this chapter. Second, some of the newer forms of jigging incorporate traditional techniques, to one degree or another. In order to get the entire picture, we need to make sure everyone's on the same page when it comes to "traditional" jigging. So, here we go.

Essentially, jigging is lowering a lure to the approximate depth of the fish, then raising and lowering your rod tip to impart a life-like action to your lure. Whether you do this slowly or quickly depends on the type of fish you're after and how active they are. In the case of weakfish, for example, on some days you may want to jerk like there's no tomorrow (warm water and high current situations) or on others you may want to hold your rod more or less still (cool water and no current; this tactic is usually called "dead-sticking"). Which of these diametric opposite tactics will work may change from day to day and situation to situation, so jigging is highly variable. How high you'll raise and lower your rod tip also varies quite a bit, with

Raise and lower your rod tip from the water to 10 o'clock.

one caveat: never raise your rod tip over the 10 o'clock position. Do so, and you'll be completely unable to set the hook if a fish strikes when you're at the top of the swing.

In fast-drop situations, those in which you'll want that jig zooming towards the bottom as quickly as possible, (which includes most situations when you have relatively active fish,) there are two schools of thought when it comes to lowering your rod tip. Some people believe you should drop fast enough that your line goes completely slack. This allows you to watch your line as it sinks. If fish hit as the jig falls, you can visibly see that the line has stopped falling, and bring your rod tip up to set the hook.

Other people like to drop their rod tip as quickly as possible without allowing any slack to form in the line, maintaining minimal tension on it at all times. This allows you to feel the strike as the jig falls, and bring your rod tip up to set the hook. Who's right, the feelers or the lookers? We could argue about it all day. I'm a feeler, because I think I'm able to react more quickly to strikes when I maintain tension on the drop. Plus, there's a risk of tip-wrapping when you allow slack into the line. But try doing each and decide which is "best" for yourself — I know excellent anglers who do it both ways.

When you arrive on-scene over a school of tunas versus a school of stripers versus a school of amberjack, how will you know how fast to jig? We'll get into specific species and what they tend to like later, but the most important thing for any angler to remember is that you should vary your technique until you figure out what works best. If fast isn't working then try going slow, and vise-versa.

\ There are no hard and fast rules as to the where's and when's of jigging. You can try this tactic any time fish are schooled up, either in open water or along an edge, break, or other form of underwater structure. Jigging does require a decent fishfinder and an operator who knows how to read it, although there are some old-timers out there who fish inshore waters and can position a boat over some form of structure they're intimately familiar with, by simply looking at distant landmarks.

Vertical jigging is most effective when fish are schooled up and it also works quite well for catching larger than average fish, when average fish are on top busting water and larger ones lurk below. Since you'll be more or less vertically positioned over the fish, it's important for the captain to be able to locate them and either position and hold the boat over the school, or position the boat for a drift over the school. He'll have to be able to accurately gauge the effects of wind and current, and judge where to park to get the perfect drift.

Captain's Tip: Chartplotters are invaluable for this purpose—I regularly discover that mine's a lot smarter than I am. Allow your boat to drift for a few minutes with the chartplotters' track function activated, then zoom in to the closest level your plotter allows. You'll see exactly what direction your boat's been moving in, and then will be able to motor into proper position to drift accordingly.

Since the fish need to be schooled to effectively jig them up, this tactic is not usually applied to species that are loners. When fish are in mobile pods or the schools are moving around a lot on an edge or break, however, jigging is one of the most effective methods you can possibly use because it allows you to maintain your mobility and constantly remain on the hunt. You may find this situation on a long, uninterrupted channel edge, or in open water when there are fast-moving pockets of bait scattered around. In these situations jigging is the best way to get a lure presented to the fish the moment you locate them on the fishfinder, without getting bogged down with bait, anchors, setting spreads, and the like. As soon as the fish move on you can, too, without any break-down time. And remember this one cardinal rule of jigging, which is true for all forms of jigging, not just traditional vertical: **don't just drift around and jerk your rod — you've got to hunt for the fish and drop your jig in front of them.** It's awful hard to get the fish to bite when they're somewhere else, and the biggest mistake most people make is to keep their lines down long after they've drifted past the structure or school they were targeting. Maintain your mobility, and keep a close eye on the meter at all times. When you see fish be ready (and have all your anglers be ready) to drop immediately, and jig for all you're worth until the boat drifts off the fish or structure, or the fish leave. As soon as you're off the mark crank up and keep those lines up until you

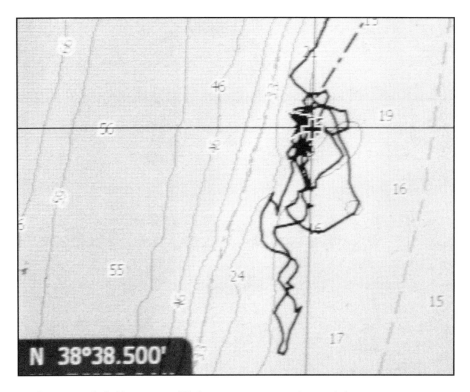

Successful jiggers will hunt constantly, with one eye on the chartplotter at all times. Drifting and hoping is usually a waste of time.

relocate more fish. Yes, you'll spend a lot of time searching if you fish this way. But at the end of the day, you'll have more fish in the cooler than the guy who drifted around and jigged the whole time, hoping to luck back into the fish.

Now that we've made a rule, naturally, there's got to be an exception: flounder. While most often flounder will be congregated on a particular edge or drop-off, you certainly can't see them on the fishfinder. (Really — you can't. I've heard guys say they can, too, and maybe I'm just missing the boat. But I've used virtually every brand fishfinder in existence and I have yet to be confident I've spotted a flounder lying on bottom.) In this case, you may find it necessary to drift around until you locate the fish by catching them. Luck for us, once you locate a specific depth the flounder are holding at, you're likely to find more at the same depth until the tide, light levels, or some other environmental factor changes.

Since we know that you'll be using that meter to locate the fish, it's obvious that you'll be able to see at a glance how deep the fish are. Yet despite this fact, one of the biggest mistakes anglers make is jigging in the wrong part of the water column. Why? Many guys just drop away, and guess at the jig's depth. Bad move. You need to know exactly where your jig is at all times, if you plan to be an effective angler.

Flounder are the exception to the rule - you won't see these fish on the meter.

The easiest way to track depth is to count line by the sweep of your rod. Here's what I mean: every time you sweep your rod tip from the water's surface up to 10 o'clock with the reel in freespool and line freely coming out, you'll be pulling a certain amount of line off of your reel. Learn how much this is. Put your jig on the swim platform of your boat or rest it on a trim tab, release line as you raise your rod tip, then measure how much you've let out with a tape measure. With most rods, it'll be somewhere between seven and nine feet of line (depending on the length of the rod, your arms, and how high off the water the deck of your boat is). When you're ready to deploy your jig, instead of merely dropping away, sweep that rod tip. At the top of the arc slip your finger around the line to hold it (or thumb the spool, when using conventional gear), and drop the rod tip until tension returns to your line. Then simultaneously release the line and sweep that tip back up again. Count the number of sweeps you let out, do some simple math, and you'll know exactly how much line you have over the side. Every so often confirm your calculations by dropping until you hit bottom, or by dropping next to the boat's transducer so you can watch your jig on the fishfinder screen. By keeping track of exactly how deep you are with this method, you'll eventually be able to do the sweep-and-drop with confidence that you can place your jig exactly where you want it in the water column — right in front of the fish's nose.

What gear is best for vertical jigging? That depends somewhat on which style of jigging you subscribe to. If you're a slack line watcher, you'll want a very fast action rod with plenty of beef in the tip, which allows you to bring that tip up and set the hook quickly. If you're an angler who likes to maintain a tensioned line and feel the bite, however, a slower tip is in order. In this case some bend is a good thing. The flexing tip will make it a heck of a lot easier to maintain tension at all times because if you drop a bit too fast, the tip will straighten a bit and take up some of the slack for you.

Reel choice is entirely up to the angler, with one caveat: it must have infinite anti-reverse. If your reel doesn't, it'll kick back as you apply and relieve pressure by jigging. Some reels, like the old stand-by Penn SS series, which are excellent for many fishing applications (I have a half-dozen of them myself), are a prime example of reels that will kick back while jigging. Even though these reels are well-built, the constant banging against the anti-reverse mechanism will eventually take a toll. Another that should be avoided are spinning reels with live-lining levers, like the Shimano Bait-runner or Penn Live-Liner. Click over that lever by accident while jigging and watch out — you're in for a serious tangle.

One thing that all experienced jiggers agree on: braid line is a must-have. Thanks to the way it cuts through the water it will speed your sink-rate. Because of the absence of stretch it will increase your jig's action and boost your hook-setting power. And since braid's sensitivity is far better then that of monofilament, you'll feel it when fish so much as sniff at your jig. If, that is, you have tension on your line.

Braid is a must-have, for serious jiggers.

Which braid is best? It's a matter of personal preference for the most part. Any of the high-end braids like Power Pro or Fireline will work great. The "fused" braids are a short step behind, as they have a bit more drag through the water and are a bit tougher to knot effectively. Regardless of which one you choose, remember to ALWAYS tie a Palomar knot when attaching terminal tackle. Improved clinches will slip and slide in braid, regardless of how many twists you put into them, while a Palomar will always hold tight. The other knot you'll need to know when fishing braid is a Spider Hitch; see the section on knots in Chapter 6, for information on how to tie each, and note that we'll go much deeper into detail about braids, knots, and rigging later on, in that chapter.

Lures used for vertical jigging range widely. The classic choice is a hammered-metal or molded lead jig with a single treble hook mounted on the aft end. Colors run the gamut, as do sizes. If you're vertically jigging for bluefin tunas you're probably swinging a six to 12 ounce jig, and if you're going for weakfish, it might be a mere two ounces. How will you know which size to choose? As a general rule of thumb, use the lightest jig that accurately mimics the bait the fish are feeding on, and lets you jig in a vertical fashion without your line being pulled off by

A selection of traditional jigging spoons. The top three are hammered metal; the bottom jig is a clear-coated Maria.

the current and drift. Constantly jigging with heavy metal gets tiring, and using a light-weight jig will allows you to stay on top of your game for longer periods of time.

Some other anglers prefer to use soft plastics for vertical jigging, and they certainly have their place in relatively shallow (under 40') water. Fish tend to hold onto them longer then metal, affording you more opportunity to set the hook, and using plastics also allows you to put scent into your arsenal.

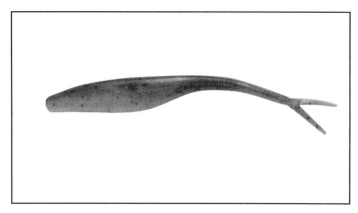

Scented soft plastics like this GULP! Jerk shad are killers.

One jig that isn't incredibly effective for vertical jigging is a jig that was designed for speed jigging. What I'm really talking about here is really the top-hook rigging — use this style for vertical jigging, and you'll soon realize that you miss an extraordinary number of hits. Picture that jig, falling through the water column. The lighter hook will be fluttering at the end of its leader, well above the jig itself. When a fish strikes the jig stops falling, and you swing your rod. Instead of burying in the fish's jaws, the hook ends up sticking in the fish's head, or gill plate. Vertically jig for bluefin with top hook only speed jigs, for example, and my logs show that you'll experience a 10–to-one strike to kill ratio. It doesn't get much worse then that! The problem became clear when a hook pulled five or six minutes into a fight, and we reeled in a chunk of a gill plate. Then, we boated a scale… we were hooking the fish alright, just not inside their jaws. Yep, you guessed it: a treble hook mounted on the bottom of the jig did the trick, and 10-to-one ratio dropped to a more acceptable three-to-one.

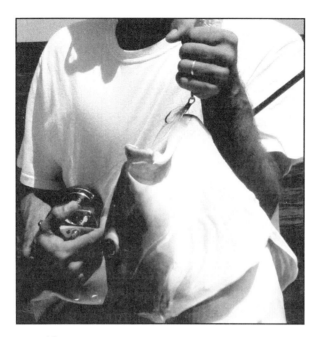

Many pro's will disagree, but experience proves that a treble on the back of a modern speed jig can come in quite handy in certain situations.

So, why would anyone in their right mind use the top hook rigging? First off, you have to remember what we stated up front: speed jigging really is quite different from the same-old, same-old jigging we're used to, and when speed jigging, this form of rigging works best. Secondly, when vertically jigging over a wreck or reef with lots of hang-ups, you may want to go to top-hook rigging because it does wonders for relieving the number of snags you'll get. Yes, you will miss a lot of bites. But the time you'll save on re-rigging alone makes top-hook rigs a winner in this case, too.

Angler's Tip

If you're using a top hook only jig because you're jigging on hard, snaggly structure, but short-striking fish are missing the hook, you can add a single hook to the bottom of the jig and hold it amidships on the jig by wrapping a rubber band around it. It'll take time to re-set the rig after every hit, but it will turn some of those missed strikes into solid hook-ups.

Chapter 2: The Motion of the Ocean – Speed Jigging

It took well over two hours, but eventually this fat bluefin tuna felt the gaff. He was taken on a nine-inch pink Butterfly jig, while speed jigging.

Believe it or not — and remember, I had a hard time accepting this myself — speed jigging really is a very different form of fishing, when compared to traditional jigging. In fact, the action of the jig moving through the water is really closer to that of a hyperactive crankbait than it is to a vertically-jigged spoon. Watch a Butterfly (or some of the many knock-offs) and you'll see that jig swerve to port, dive, dart back up, zig to starboard, then zag in any given direction, all as it moves forward at a fast rate of speed. Net result: predators that see it moving erratically through the water are triggered into action.

If the action's closer to a swimming bait then a jig, why not use a swimming bait to attain it? Because there are several major-league advantages to having a speed jigging rig in your hands. First off, speed jigging allows you to more or less cover the entire water column. If fish are at 50' you can drop to 60' then retrieve through them. If they're on the surface you can keep the lure up high. And as they appear on the fishfinder at any given depth you can constantly let line out and sink, or rip the jig in and get it up higher, as need be, in a matter of moments. With a crankbait — or a skirted 'hoo, a spreader bar, or the vast majority of other lures you could be using to try and tempt the very same fish — you'll have to pick a depth (or zero depth) and set it there with weight, line length, speed, and any number of factors that require additional time and adjustments. Basically, although the tactics are different this particular

Flexibility in your ability to target different species in different settings is a key advantage of speed jigging.

advantage of speed jigging is very similar to that held by other forms of jigging: you retain flexibility and mobility. You can change depths, speeds, and targeted areas with very little time investment or effort. Added bonus: you can even change techniques. If you're speed jigging for tunas and you happen to pass over a spot where you see a pile of sea bass hugging a strip of hard bottom, for example, you can drop the speed jig down and give it a vertical jigging action to catch those fish. Or, maybe you just floated by a board filled with mahi-mahi. Crank up that jig, toss it past the flotsam, whip it by, and you've suddenly added another species to the box. Wait a sec — toss it past the board? Yes, that's right, another advantage of using speed jigging gear is that most rigs designed for this type of fishing can be cast. Now picture trolling with a 30-wide or a 50, which you might otherwise be using for a day of offshore fishing if you're targeting big game. This type of rig is far, far more limiting. And if you feel that variety is the spice of life, so much the better because jiggers are often treated to surprises that trollers working the top section of the water column, only, will never get to see. Since you can probe from bottom to the surface, you simple never know what's going to inhale your jig — or get impaled by it!

You just never know what's going to hit a speed jig... or get hit by it!

Like they say on TV: but wait, there's more! Speed jigging also allows you to target extremely large fish with gear so light it's mind-blowing. This is, to a great degree, thanks to modern technology. And we'll dig deeper into this in just a moment when we examine specific jigging gear. But first, let's check out the technique of speed jigging itself.

The first departure from the normal jigging motion is also the most dramatic —

Sure, size matters. But as fishing buddy Josh Lowery proves, relatively small modern gear can pack a heck of a punch. The peashooter he holds is spooled with 120-pound braid and can put out 35 pounds of drag.

there is none of the sweep up/sweep down motion that we all know and love. Rather, it's a drop, then reel-and-pump motion. Both port and starboard hands lift up and drop down at the same time, with the right hand (assuming you're a rightie) setting the pace by reeling. And that pace should be as quick as possible without throwing the right and left hands out of kilter. The left hand simply follows the same circular motion, at the same time as the right hand goes round and round. Since your left hand is supporting the rod, this causes it to lift vertically, as opposed to pivoting on a diagonal axis. Meanwhile, the rod butt is tucked into your arm pit; properly designed jigging rods have exceptionally long butts, for just this purpose.

Unlike virtually every other form of jigging your hands are not used as a pivot point for the rod, and the rod should remain more or less on the same vertical plane, parallel to the boat's deck, the entire time you speed jig. The lifting motion is just that — lifting, not swinging — so the rod tip never goes above nine o'clock nor below eight o'clock. Your right hand, all the while, should be cranking just as fast as you can make it go. Part of the reason speed jigging works is because the jig's darting motion triggers a reaction strike from predators, and if you try and do it slowly the fish will react with a yawn. That's why speed jigging reels are made with massive gears, featuring outrageous retrieve ratios. Take a Shimano Torsa, for example, since these were some of the first bluewater-capable reels designed purely for speed jigging. (And, by the way, are the sweetest reels you'll ever hold in your hands.) The Torsa has a 5.8:1 retrieve ratio, which means you'll be retrieving 45" of line every time you rotate the handle one crank. Now remember, you'll be cranking it as fast as you can while still keeping up the motion; for most of us that'll mean you crank about three- quarters of full-tilt. At this rate you can get that handle around twice in a second, which means your jig is moving along at quite a nice clip — about eight feet per second.

The Torsa brings in 45" of line with every revolution of the crank.

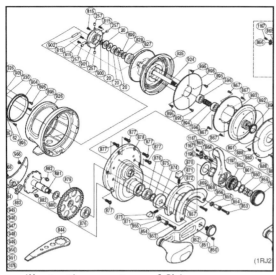

Huge gears, beefy drags, and high-quality construction is absolutely necessary if you're going to take on large fish with light speed jigging gear. Don't go cheap - invest in the best reels possible.

Illustration courtesy of Shimano

Warning: at first, this technique will feel really clumsy. But after an hour or so, you'll get the hang of it. And you'll know you've got it perfect when the tip of your rod loads and unloads as you crank. Even though the rod is parallel to the water, this motion will cause the tip to bend deeply, then spring back to shape — and this is a great deal of what gives the speed jig that incredibly erratic motion.

Angler's Tip

It can be tough to envision a motion described in words, so you might want to go to www.butterflyfishing.com. There you'll find a set of videos that show how it's done. Take the commentary with a grain of salt (it is, after all, produced by Shimano) because there's a lot of product marketing going on. But it's worth watching to get a view of the action. Youtube has jigging videos both good and bad; a good one is called "High Speed Vertical Jigging" by "Flatslam". Suffer through the talking at the beginning and you'll see a good demonstration of the motion.

It should be noted that plenty of highly-effective anglers speed jig in a manner that a speed jigging purist would call "wrong," yet they catch the heck out of fish. I've seen guys who essentially vertically jig while reeling, guys who reel while ripping the rod left then right, and guys who use a jig-reel-jig technique. And later in this book, in the chapters on targeting specific species, you'll find sections where I describe combinations of these motions and others — that's right, I like mutating the "correct" motions too. Bottom line: who cares what is "correct," if you're slamming the fish? That's another one of the beauties of speed jigging; it allows you to try different rhythms, speeds, and retrieval styles, any of which could prove to be the most effective on any given day. So while you should practice this textbook speed jigging technique, later on you should be willing to change it, tweak it, and experiment with it in specific ways for specific species in specific situations. I absolutely guarantee that in many cases, it'll be a radical departure from the norm that fills the cooler.

Even combined with this "new" jigging motion, standard rods and reels simply can't get your lure moving the same way that gear designed specifically for this purpose does. You already know that speed jigging reels must be fast, so let's stick with the Torsa example for the time being. They differ from common conventional reels in many ways other then their beefed up gears and lightening-fast retrieves. First off, their drags are on par with true big-game reels like Tiagras or Internationals, and can be cranked up to put some serious heat on a fish; 30 pounds of pressure is no problem. That may not sound like a lot, but think of the general drag-setting rule of thumb. Most anglers set their drags between 25- and 30-percent of the line's rated breaking strength. That means that a 50 set at 18 pounds of pressure is on the heavy side. If you've ever tussled with a tuna on a 50, you know that this feels like enough pressure to yank your feet right off the deck — so imaging just how much oomph you've got when the reel's set to 30-pounds!

Another advantage many of these reels hold over others is that they are available in narrow-spool versions (usually denoted by the "N" at the end of the model number). Narrow-spool reels of this size don't require level-winding — the line just lays naturally down, back and forth, as you retrieve. When you're putting every ounce of energy you have into turning the crank and holding the rod up, that's a huge advantage. Of course, there's also a down-side to this feature. Narrow-spool reels don't have the line capacity of wider-spool reels, and when spooled with 80-lb. braid, A 16N will be pushing the limits when fishing for big game in depths over 300' or so. If you plan to target large pelagics in deep water, you may need to either opt for a larger reel or drop line size as a result.

Rods also are an important (imperative!) part of speed jigging. We'll get into them in more depth in Chapter Five: Jigging Gear – Rods and Reels, but for now we at least need to know that simply using any old rod will not do. You need a rod that's incredibly light and strong, but more importantly has a tip that's very flexible. Enough so, in fact, that the weight of a jig puts a significant bend into the first foot of the rod. The middle and rear sections of the rod should grow progressively stiffer as you move aft, with enough overall lifting power to crank up one of your outboards. The action throughout the rod also needs to

Note the different arc in the jigging rod (left) versus the traditional stand-up rod (right).

be fast — unlike a rod used for vertical jigging, where a slow action is advantageous to those using the tight-line technique. When you combine the action of the rod, the crank-and-lift motion, the fast reel, and the shaped speed jig together, you get that quick darting, bobbing, weaving motion that activates predators. Added Bonus: when a fish takes the lure you're always ready to set the hook no matter what stage of the jigging motion you happen to be in. In most scenarios, you won't even have time to set the hook because the fish will smash the lure at high speed like a ton of bricks, doing the job for you.

When is speed jigging appropriate? Any time fish are schooled and suspended, this is a killer tactic. Tunas hanging just below a thermocline are a prime example. Often a thermocline — the point at which two layers of differing water temperatures meet — will form in the inshore waters off the Mid Atlantic coast, somewhere between 40' and 80' down, in depths ranging from 100' to 300'. Find a lump 20 to 50 miles off the beach within this depth range (during the correct time of year, of course), and you've got a fair chance of locating tunas. Look at the depths around the thermocline in an area like this, and you'll note that quite often, the fish are hanging just above or below it.

Captain's Tip

To locate the thermocline, turn the gain on your fishfinder to manual. Then slowly but constantly increase it, until you get a faint reading somewhere in the middle section of the water column. This is the thermocline; your depth finder can "see" it because different temperature water has different density, and because plankton gathers at the barrier between the two differing bodies of water.

Say that thermocline is at 70'. There's a very good chance you'll see tuna marks at 75' to 80'. These usually won't be massive schools of fish, but pods of five or 10. You may see a nice grouping on the meter, or you might only see two or three marks. In either case, those fish are orienting to the thermocline. If you've been searching in the proper direction — into the prevailing wind/current force, but more on this tactic later — and are prepared to drop, do so as soon as you see those marks. If not, you'll have to try to spin on the fish and get your boat set up properly.

Since these fish are at a specific depth you'll have to do a measured drop; just letting out line until you guess the jig is deep enough simply doesn't cut it. Do so with those sweeps of your rod tip we discussed earlier. Of course, when you're letting out line you won't want to stop the lure from sinking every time you sweep the rod, or it'll delay your lure's decent. But with a bit of practice, you'll quickly get used to dropping the rod tip immediately after a sweep, watching the line as it sinks, and then starting a new sweep just as it comes taut.

Let's say that in your case, one sweep is seven feet. Now, you know that every sweep of the rod tip will bring out seven feet of line, and can measure your drops accordingly. Sweep the tip 11 times, and you'll have 77' of line out. That may be the depth those tuna marks are at, but don't stop just yet. The amount of line you've let out doesn't necessarily equate the depth your lure is at because of water pressure against the line, created as your boat drifts. Now, you'll also have to account for the angle of the line that's being created. Here things get a bit fuzzy. It would be nice to say there's a hard and set rule as to how to judge a specific line angle and know exactly how much additional line you need to release to hit the target depth, but truth be told, you'll have to use your best judgment to make an educated guess. As a rule of thumb, remember that when your line's at a 45-degree angle off the boat, your lure is only half as deep as the amount of line you've let out.

Gauging the depth of your jig accurately is imperative. With your line at a 45-degree angle, you'll have to let out twice the distance to the target depth.

There are two ways you can verify that your lure is at the target depth. First off, take your best guess at the target zone, and then continue letting out additional sweeps (and continue keeping count of how much line you're letting out) until the jig hits bottom; then do the math to "audit" your judgment of what depth the lure was at. The second way to confirm you've got the right depth? When a fish slams the jig.

Let's say that at this point you've accurately judged the depth of your drop, and your jig is exactly where the fish are. Now drop it some more. When speed jigging you want that lure to start out well below the fish. Remember, unlike vertical jigging, you're not trying to place the jig in front of the fish's face and dance it around. Instead you're going to get that jig moving and zing it past the fish, triggering the reaction strike. To do so, you'll want to drop a good 10' or 20' below the fish before you start your retrieve, at least. You'll want the jig moving at full-tilt when it goes by the fish, and when the fish aren't more then

Get your jig well below the depth of suspended fish, before speed jigging it back past them.

50' off the bottom, it's often best to simply drop your jig all the way, and start cranking after touch-down.

OK: You've located the tunas hanging at 75' just below the thermocline. You shifted into neutral just as you spotted the fish on the meter, got those jigs over the side fast, and counted sweeps to place your jig at a depth of 90'. You lock up the reel, tuck the rod butt under your arm, and start the crank-and-lift at top speed. On the fourth turn of the handle, WHAM! Thank goodness you had a death-grip on that rod because now it's doubled over and line is flying off the reel at Ludicrous Speed. Let 'em run, you can't stop the initial surge of a 100 pound-plus bluefin without breaking something. 150 yards of spectra later, he'll calm down. Good. Now do the pump-and-crank, and bring that big boy in. Half an hour later the gaff strikes home and hot-damn, we're going to be grilling tuna steaks for a month. Congratulations—you've just become addicted to speed jigging.

A new addict is born.

Chapter 3: Meet the Jiggers – Meat Jigging

The best vindication of your fishin' addiction is a cooler packed full of fish. And after my first experience meat jigging, there was no questioning the value of this particular tactic — we had a 110-quart Rigid Frigid cooler in the back of the pickup, loaded down with wreckfish, sea bass, and tilefish. Sure, we'd had a four hour drive to the dock, followed by a four hour cruise to the canyon. But then we enjoyed a solid seven hours of fishing… before starting the eight-hour trek back home. And of course, there was some added time spent cleaning the fish.

Brandon Honeycutt, of Jerkthatjig, displays a wreckfish as fishing buddy Matt Boomer fights a second one.

Was it worth forgoing sleep for 26 hours? Hell yes — I'd pull off the same psychotic trip again in a heartbeat, and after fighting dozens of fish up into the 40-pound class, I'll bet you'd do it, too. Ready to roll? Then let's go meat jigging.

Meat jigging is a technique that's most effective for bottom dwelling fish found in deep water (300' or more) over hard or live bottom, but not necessarily a wreck or other form of structure that sticks off the bottom. Some good examples include tilefish, both goldens and blues, which will be found in 300' to 800' over relatively smooth bottom (go deeper for goldens and shallower for blues - more on that later,) and wreckfish holding around hard bottom in the 500' to 600' range. You'll also likely pick up an assortment of smaller fish like sea bass and black-belly rosies while meat jigging in these depths.

Why not just use bait for these fish? Wouldn't that be more effective? In a word, no. First off, when you drop one of those bait rigs you'll often hook a half-pound black-belly rosy or a hake, which means reeling all the way back up to get the little

As fishing buddy John Unkart shows, with a meat-curtain rig lots of time may be spent cleaning little nippers off your line. These rosies are about twice as big as most fish John catches.

fish off your hook so you can re-bait and get another shot at a whopper. Meanwhile, regular deep dropping with a heavily-weighted "meat-curtain" rig can also be a real drag simply by virtue of the work it takes to reel it up. A fruitless drift through 600' of water followed by cranking up three or four pounds of lead isn't exactly thrilling. That makes one wonder if deep-drop vertical jigging wouldn't be a better idea. Dropping and reeling in the jig is less tiresome then cranking lead, (though keeping a 12-ounce jig in motion at all times is also quite a workout), and big jigs will be more or less left alone by fish too small to be interesting. In waters over 300' deep, however, where light is minimal, bare jigs are clearly less effective then a slew of hooks baited up with fish and squid chunks. The ultimate solution to the bait-versus-jig deep-dropping question? A combination of both methods: meat jigging.

A Jerkthatjig, sweetened with a glob of meat, put this wreckfish into feeding mode.

This technique has been pioneered by the father-son fishing team of Donald and Brandon Honeycutt, the owners of Jerkthatjig jigs, and they were the catalyst that brought my first meat jigging trip, a run from Hampton, VA to the Norfolk Canyon, into being. I went on this trip expecting to test out their lures—a unique selection of jigs that includes some two pound models, which is double the weight of most "mega" jigs. What I didn't expect was an introduction to a whole different style of jigging.

The basic technique is quite simple, but has several unusual components starting with the 750-gram monster Jerkthatjig which tapes out at over 10" long, an inch and a half wide, and half an inch thick. Any jig will work for meat-jigging, by the way, though you'll have trouble locating other brands of this size. These are the biggest jigs in town, literally twice the size of most company's largest models, and they're so thick and heavy you could club a bear to death with one of these things — literally. The jig comes pre-rigged with an 8/0 hook at the top, Butterfly style. The hook's attached to a solid ring which is linked up with the jig via a split ring. Also note the strip of glow paint running down the edges of the jig; in the low-light environment, any light-producing lure is a plus.

Tackle is essentially standard jigging fare. The Honeycutts specifically like a Shimano Torium 30 on a Tallus rod, such as the TLC66H fast action model with Fuji Hardloy guides. Line

Jerkthatjig's 750-gram monster jig.

is 60 to 80 pound test braid, topped off with an 80-pound test fluorocarbon leader. The fluoro can be attached either via a loop-to-loop connection by tying a Spider Hitch or a Bimini Twist in the two ends, or you can do a loop-to-loop with a pre-made wind-on leader. I used this rig, as well as a Shimano Torsa reel/Trevala rod and a Penn Torque reel/Falcon rod combo, and found all worked well for meat-jigging. The speed of the reel isn't

Grouper is another deepwater species that slurps up meat jigging.

as imperative as it is for speed jigging since you're not using a fast retrieve to get the jig's action, although you do still want a speedy reel because it make for less time spent cranking. And when you're dropping in very deep water, this is no small matter because winding up with a slow reel can take five to 10 minutes more then it will with a super-fast reel. More important than the reel is the soft jigging rod tip, for reasons we'll talk about in just a moment.

Before dropping, the jig gets baited up with a chunk of squid or a strip of fish. Tipping with bait is usually verboten when speed, vertical, or yo-yo jigging, because the bait often ruins the action of the jig. (If you feel the stink of bait is necessary to draw strikes when using these techniques you should probably be using a lure like a bucktail, which is forward-weighted and thus isn't thrown out of kilter with a chunk of fish or crab threaded onto the hook.) Since we

Note the size of the meat chunks hanging out of these fish's mouths - don't be shy about going big with the bait when meat jigging.

are going to bait up for meat jigging, however, many anglers would cut a pennant of squid or a thin strip of fish, thread it on the hook, and hope it's enough to attract predators without interfering with the action of the jig too darn much. That's not how meat jigging works. This technique doesn't call for a pennant or a strip — we're talking about a big, honking chunk. A fist-sized slab of mackerel, or a glob of squid big enough to choke on. Don't forget that the jig is huge too, so all things considered the giant bait isn't really out of line. Once you've dropped your meat-laden jig down to the bottom, forget all about the standard sweep-and-drop motion we vertical jiggers know and love. And, forget about the crank-and-lift of speed jigging. Instead, the angler gently raises his rod tip, then lowers it until the jig just ticks off the bottom. The jig is allowed to sit for a few seconds, before the rod tip is raised again. Now wait. Pause with the jig suspended off bottom and simply let the motion of the boat combined with the bend of the soft rod tip impart all of the action that jig is getting for a few moments. Then drop it to the bottom again and start the lift and pause all over again. Large bottom dwellers like wreckfish, blueline tilefish, and grouper will usually smash the jig as it bobs around just off the bottom, slowly rising and falling. Again, the key here is to bounce off bottom, raise the jig, and *allow the boat* to provide the jig's motion. It's a presentation akin to dead-sticking for weakfish, albeit in 600' or more of water. And this is why we mentioned earlier that soft rod tip is so important. In oceanic swell, the rising and falling of the boat combined with the flexibility of the tip and the no-stretch braid line, gives the jig an enticing slow action which — when combined with the smell and taste of the bait chunk — seems to trigger attacks from ambush predators, like these aforementioned species.

Got the action down-pat? Good deal. Now, make sure you keep it slow enough that those small bottom fish can keep up with you. Remember what a problem those little nippers could be with baited rigs? When meat jigging, they're actually an asset. While at the Norfolk that day with the Honeycutts, the areas we were fishing were literally riddled with black-belly rosies. We had one test-fishing "control" angler onboard, using a standard deep-drop bait rig the entire time so we could compare results. He hooked (and had to crank up) rosie after rosie after rosie. Yes, these are tasty fish. But when you're targeting grouper and wreckfish the last thing you want to do is spend all day reeling in half-pound fish, re-baiting, and re-dropping. And by the time four jiggers had put their 20 and 30 pound wreckfish into the box, the bait angler had nothing larger than two pounds

Rosies are good eating and fun to catch, but... do you really want to reel up four pounds of lead and a multi-hook rig for 800', just to get this little guy into the boat? (Tiny fish for photograph provided courtesy of John Unkart.)

to show for his efforts. I've seen this time and time again, while deep dropping in 750' for goldens ("...dang it, I have to reel it all the way in again for another _@$* little rosy!?!") and while fishing cut fish for grouper ("...no, don't bother getting the net."). How does the jig turn those little nippers into an advantage? Small fish will bite at the bait on the jig, but since it's so big they'll rarely be able to inhale the entire thing and get hooked. When you feel 'em go ahead and attempt a hook-set, even though you suspect it's just a small nibbler. That will jerk the bait and lure away, forcing the small fish to back off, swim around, and (in all likelihood) come back around to take another snap at it. Larger fish, meanwhile, are attracted to your jig by the commotion of the little guys darting around. They'll then see the big jig and the meat fluttering around, and move in for the kill. You'll notice that quite often you'll feel a few nibblers and shake them free of the jig, then moments later feel the jarring strike of a more significant predator.

Added bonus: those 750-gram jigs hit bottom in 600' in about a minute, while standard deep-drop rigs with multiple baited hooks take almost twice as long. And with a bait rig, if the fish strip off the meat you'll sit there bite-less, wondering why you're not getting any strikes until you crank up and re-bait. But with the jig on the end of your line you always have a shot at getting hit, even if the bait's been stripped away.

The results of a good day of meat jigging at the Norfolk.

Chapter 4: No Child's Play– Yo-yoing

Bailing mahi-mahi from around lobster floats and other flotsam is a ton of fun, but you usually only catch relatively small fish in this way…right? Sort of, but on the *Project Boat*, running out of Ocean City, Maryland, we'd catch plenty of fish in the 15 to 50 pound class while bailing — thanks to the yo-yo technique.

At the time, we didn't even realize that's what we were doing. In fact, these big mahi weren't even the target fish. My mate at the time was convinced that if he tossed out a heavy, shiny "wahoo bomb" each and every time we approached a float, eventually, he'd catch a wahoo. More often, however, big mahi chased his lure to

Dropping bombs for wahoo…

…usually leads to big mahi, instead.

53

the surface. In fact, he never did get an attack from one of those toothy 'hoo – but he did attract a heck of a lot of nice dolphin this way.

When you locate a large school of chicken dolphin in the two to 10 pound range, which is the common catch around the balls, larger fish are often lurking below. If you only bail near the surface you might miss a half a dozen of these big boys in a day, and never even know it. The trick to catching them is teasing 'em up to the surface.

The traditional yo-yo technique, which in some ways was a precursor to speed jigging, is as simple as it gets: Throw out a jig, let it sink to bottom, then crank like mad until it's back at the boat. This is what the packaging on the wahoo bomb said to do, so this is what my mate did. And every so often a big, hot mahi would follow the lure right up to the surface. Interestingly, they never hit the jig. But, that was perfectly fine with me. Since we were bailing, when the fish got close to the surface

Californians commonly go on the yo-yo when fishing for yellowtail.
(Photo courtesy of Ran Ballanti)

they'd see our chunks sinking through the water and go into a full-tilt feeding frenzy. I don't recall a single fish ever getting hooked on the Bomb, but plenty of our guests swinging their bailing rods hooked into big fish that the Bomb drew up from the depths. In other situations or with other lures, like those Californians going after yellowtail, yo-yoing will produce plenty of strikes. But for an east coast angler it's a tactic worth understanding if for no other reason then to bring those big mahi up from the depths, .

Now let's take the simple, and make it a tad more complex. Although yo-yoing is about as easy to understand as turning the handle on a reel, there are a few nuances you need to be aware of.

For starters, when yo-yoing you'll want to allow the jig to free-fall to get it down to the bottom as quickly as possible. This mandates watching your line closely the whole time that jig's sinking, in case a fish strikes it as it falls. If you're not in tune with how your line's zipping through the water, you might never even notice. If it suddenly ceases falling, lock the reel up, bring in any slack as quickly as possible, and swing for the stars to set that hook.

You've spotted some flotsam with fish underneath? Time to go yo-yo.

Another thing you'll want to keep in mind is keeping your rod tip down low, more or less in line with your fishing line, as you retrieve. You'll hook more of the strikes that you get while the jig comes up by simply continuing to crank, then you will by swinging the rod. If your rod's at nine o'clock as you retrieve, for example, and you get a strike, there will be a lot of bend in the tip before the force gets to the end of your fishing line and drives the hook home. But with the tip pointed directly

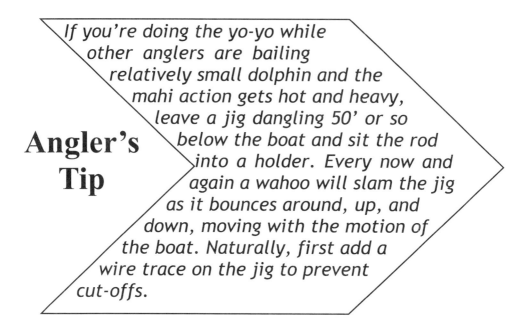

Angler's Tip

If you're doing the yo-yo while other anglers are bailing relatively small dolphin and the mahi action gets hot and heavy, leave a jig dangling 50' or so below the boat and sit the rod into a holder. Every now and again a wahoo will slam the jig as it bounces around, up, and down, moving with the motion of the boat. Naturally, first add a wire trace on the jig to prevent cut-offs.

at the lure there's a direct transfer of power from the reel to the hook (we're assuming here that you're using no-stretch braid line, of course,) and simply cranking full-tilt will drive the hook home.

As your jig nears the end of the retrieve, keep your focus on the water. Remember – particularly with mahi around flotsam, you'll often have a follow as opposed to a real take. In this situation you'll want to have another offering ready to put over the side, as well as some fish chunks or peanut bunker for chum. If you spot a fish eyeballing the jig, yell for another angler to toss the chunks over the side and then get a baited hook into the water. (Any cut fish or squid, or whole ballyhoo, work well for this purpose. If you have livies, so much the better.) When lots of small dolphin are in the area and it's tough to get a bait to the big boy before a small fish slurps it up, rig your largest bailing rod with a whole ballyhoo hooked through the jaws or eyes. Small fish will have a tough time choking this down and usually leave it alone, while the big mahi will attack it with glee.

Back to yo-yoing: if you feel a bump during the retrieve on a yo-yo drop, the natural response is to stop reeling. Don't. And, don't try re-dropping. If this happens just keep on cranking, and there's a good chance you'll keep the fish hot and get another strike on the way up. Re-drop, and there's a better chance the fish will lose interest in your offering.

Despite my mate's poor luck, note that yo-yoing will produce strikes from wahoo in areas where they frequent. (They were few and far between when he was doing this, as it was always a bit early in the season for them. As a teacher, he had to return to school by the time the wahoo showed up in our neck of the woods — yet another example of work interfering with fishing. Bummer!) If you expect good numbers of these fish to be around, you may want to rig six or eight inches of single-strand wire to your jig for a little extra tooth-protection.

There's one other time yo-yoing is quite effective: when stripers and/or bluefish have suspended beneath baitfish. This is quite common in bays and inlets during the fall, when schools of peanut bunker have migrated out of tributaries.

The Chesapeake offers a great example, usually during late October or early November. Bunker often hold 10' to 15' below the surface in 20' to 50' deep areas outside the tributary river mouths, and stripers move in to feed. Most anglers will look for working birds, and cast in the feeding frenzy to catch these stripers. But they don't always bust on the surface, and they often sound as boat traffic spooks the bait quite regularly. (Note to anglers fishing up top: approach these schools at idle speed, or you'll likely break up the fish and send them down!) Once these schools go beneath the surface they'll be tougher to find, but you'll sometimes spot them on your fishfinder as you mill around waiting for the fish to start breaking again. That's the time to yo-yo.

For some reason, vertical jigging through these fish won't always produces a strike. But plastics rigged to one ounce jig heads can be dropped to the bottom — remember to watch that line, because they will sometimes get struck during the fall — and then cranked straight back up. You'll want to also give a little bit of action to the jig with your rod tip with every other rotation of the crank (yes, that means it isn't a purist's form of yo-yoing, but who cares when you're catching fish?) or so. As the jig zips up through the school, the stripers will often get triggered into an attack. It's usually not imperative to crank at full-tilt in this situation, but drop to bottom then reel straight up through the school and you have a great shot at hooking up.

Chapter 5: Jigging Gear – Rods and Reels

Doesn't that view make your mouth water?

As with all types of fishing, personal preference plays a larger role then anything else when it comes to choosing jigging gear. That said, there are more special requirements when it comes to jigging tackle then there are with most other forms of fishing, especially if you plan to utilize several jigging tactics with the same rig(s). In some cases, your preference will depend on your own style of jigging. Vertical jigging is a perfect example; slack-liners will be reaching for the fast-action tip, while taunt-liners will be handling rods with much slower tips.

Before you pick out the specifics, one thing every angler should know: just reading this book, researching the topic, or any other form of information-gathering is not good enough to make the choices you'll need to make — you need to hold this stuff in your hands, feel it, and if at all possible, use it before buying it. Every person is built differently, and the rod and reel combo that feels like magic in my hands may not feel so perfect in yours. So take every opinion given in this chapter as just that—an opinion that you may or may not agree with. When it comes to specs and specifics, of course, you can learn a lot about a rod or reel. But always assemble a rod and reel combination, hold it in your hands, and try cranking, feeling pressure against the tip, and tucking the butt under your arm to get a feel for it before you decide it's the "best" one for you.

While it would be ideal to spend a day fishing with a rod and reel combo before deciding whether or not to purchase it, this simply isn't realistic for most folks. So you'll have to do the next best thing, and try it out in the tackle shop. Luckily, there are a few ways you can "test" gear even when stuck on dry land.

Rods

We're going to start with rods because it's a lot easier to pick out your rod first then match a reel to it, as opposed to going about it the other way around. You can test the action and feel of a rod before a reel goes onto it, while assessing a reel without it being mounted on a rod is nearly impossible.

Will you want a fast action rod, or a slow one? Think back to that stylistic argument, because this is what will determine your choice when it comes to vertical jigging. For nearly all other forms of jigging, however, flexible tips with a fairly fast recovery will be advantageous. You'll have to judge for yourself which aspect is most important to you, and choose accordingly.

How do you judge a rod's action in the showroom? Ideally, put a spooled reel onto it, grab a jig of a size you'd expect to be using, and tie it onto the end of the line. With the jig dangling, bounce the tip up and down to get a feel for how soft it is. If you don't have a pre-spooled reel handy, have someone hold their arm outstretched at a 90-degree angle from their body, and bring the rod tip up until it touches their hand. Apply and release pressure, to feel how flexible the tip is.

Note: Don't go crazy here, — this is not a safe way to test the strength of a rod and I have sizable divots in my livingroom ceiling to prove it.

Weight is another thing you'll want to feel for. The lighter a rod is, the easier it will be to swing it all day long. Don't take weight or diameter as a reflection of strength, though. Some offshore-capable jigging rods that can be used effectively to take large tunas and other pelagics look quite literally like striper gear. Some others that are broom-stick thick will snap under the force of 20 pounds of drag. Testing for strength itself is a tough call, as you won't find out how strong a rod is until it breaks. Snap one in half in the tackle shop, and the proprietor won't appreciate it very much. Trust me — been there, done that. However, it's worth noting that any reputable rodbuilder will normally replace rods that broke while being used, as opposed to those slammed in a car door or stepped on while they lay on the deck.

The mechanics: No matter the action or size of the jigging rod you choose, some things are must-haves. First off, make sure it has guide liners that can handle the stress of braid. Some are just called "braid safe," and some really are, but don't trust the label. Do your homework, and make sure any rod you consider has high quality guide liners which can handle the heat and stress of 80-pound Spectra zinging through them. Get the wrong rod, and you'll be dropping a $20 jig on a $100 spool of line and after 200' or 300' of free-fall, the line will suddenly snap at the tip. Most guys will wonder what the heck happened, and probably spend another $100 to re-spool the reel. Then, the very next time they go fishing, the line will part just seconds after the drop starts, sending another $20 jig to the bottom. Suspicion will now lead to a close inspection of the guides, whereupon one will discover sharp-edged grooves cut into the liners. Yep — been there and done that, too... on a $300 rod that was advertised as "braid safe."

At this point, you're probably wondering why a specific type of liner hasn't been identified as "braid safe" yet. That's because whether or not a guide will grove is dependent on a number of things, including the length of the drop, the amount of weight on the line (and how much tension is applied as it's let out), the guide liner itself, and the type of braid. In fact, I've had experiences where high-quality guides that were advertised a braid-safe became grooved on the first use, and conversely, where "cheap" guides have done just fine with braid for years on end. This is akin to judging the hauling capacity of a pick-up. The number specified by the manufacturer could turn out to be too much on the transmission if you drive up and down mountains at 75-mph, but you might also be able to go well beyond that capacity without any problems if you're towing at 10-mph on a flat straightaway. The bottom line: if any rod is under $100 and the manufacturer doesn't specify the exact type of material used in the line guides, be very, very suspicious. Generally speaking, alconite and silicon carbide liners do best, hardaloy and aluminum-oxide are good, and anything of a lesser quality will usually become toast in short order. Remember to keep tension as low as possible when dropping large weights for long distances, and check liners regularly after stressful use, by running cotton balls through them. (If they have nicks or burrs, tiny strands of cotton will get caught in them and tip you off to the damage.)

Another thing you'll want to look at on a jigging rod is the wraps. Some rods look great but lose their guides a year or two after they go into service, thanks to lightweight, machine-wrapped guide feet. To make sure a rod has decent wraps grab all of the eyes one at a time, and try to rotate them from side to side. If there's any motion at all, avoid the rod like the plague.

Also look for yellowing or cracking in the clear-coat finish on the wraps, which indicates sub-par finish that deteriorated quickly.

Should jigging rods have gimbaled butts, or rounded ends? I prefer those that are gimbaled, because I like being able to strap an angler into a harness for those long, tough fights. Ideally, the rod you choose will have a gimbaled butt that comes with an  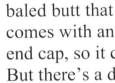 end cap, so it can be used without belts, as well. But there's a down-side to gimbaled butts in that they tend to rip vinyl seat upholsters, mark non-skid, and leave a bruise in the gut when used without a belt. If you plan on using lighter rods and reels, you simply may not find gimbaled butts necessary and may want to forego them.

Another part of the rod you'll want to inspect prior to purchase is the reel seat. Graphite and/or plastic seats are fine for most rods, but if the rod flexes all the way to the butt, they will sometimes come un-glued. There's no way I'm aware of to check a rod for this problem prior to purchase, but getting rods with aluminum seats eliminates the issue. Note: they also cost a heck of a lot more, and add weight to a rod. You'll also need to verify that the seat of any rod you're looking at will accommodate the reel you intend on matching it up with. Surprisingly, you'll sometimes discover the manufacturer used a seat too small or too large to fit the rig you want to match it up with.

Grip material is entirely up to you. Some guys like neoprene or foam, others insist that cork is better. I've never been able to rank one over the other for any specific reason.

What about the material the rod's blank itself is built from? Is graphite, fiberglass, or some combination of the two the best choice? Generally speaking, rods with higher graphite contents will have better sensitivity, but will also be more brittle and tend to snap more easily then fiberglass rods. The vast majority of the rods on the market today utilize some combination of these two materials, so neither should really be thought of as "best."

A final general note about rods, before moving on to specifics: I've seen more guys then I can count take a regular 30 or 50 class trolling rod, slap a jig on the end of the line, and start swinging. If you've tried this, you already know it's a useless endeavor. You won't get the action on your lure, you'll have zero sensitivity, and if you keep it up for half an hour you'll feel like your arms are going to fall off. Use the right tool for the job, and don't try to fake it or cheap out by using trolling gear for jigging.

Here are some specific rods, which I've found to be excellent for the forms of jigging discussed in this book and constitute my top picks for jigging sticks (listed in alphabetic order).

Chaos Jigging Rod

Chaos has a fairly new (as of the publication of this book) line of graphite/glass composite rods that look and feel like pea-shooters but have the punch of a bazooka. There are 6'6" and 7'0" models, in both spinning and conventional versions. They're the size of rods that look like they'd be rated for 17 or 20 pound test, but they're rated for 30 to 60, 60 to 80, and 80 to 100 pounds. I've fished one spooled up with 60-lb braid — these rods were developed specifically for braid — and have caught fish up to 60-pound bluefin tuna on it. It felt like it had the same backbone and lifting power as a traditional 30 to 60 pound class rod, at about half the weight and diameter.

Due to a tip action that's slightly faster and stiffer then many jigging rods, it takes some weight to get the rod to load and unload effectively and when speed jigging, and it's not effective with less then four ounces on the end of your line. Six works better. Of course, this action also means that anglers who like to vertical jig with slack line technique will find this rod ideal. The mid section blends into an aft section that has a ton of backbone. 60-pound fish, for example, don't cause any bend in the rod beyond the lowest guide.

Grips are foam, guides are the double-foot style and are lined with silicon-carbide inserts, and the reel seat is gold and black anodized aluminum. The tip top on the rod I tested, however, did groove and required replacement. (Chaos said this doesn't normally happen and mine had a bad tip. In my experience, this is a reliable company that stands behind its products so I doubt that anyone else will have this occur — but check those tip-tops to be safe.) Wraps around the guides are gold over black, and the wraps near the base are criss-crossed. The butt is gimbaled so you can use this rod with a harness, and it comes with a rubber end-piece cap so you can also fish it without one. These rods start around $200 and go up from there.

Falcon Cara T7

The Falcon Cara T7 is medium-light spinning rod designed specifically for low-diameter braid. I regularly use a 6'6" CS-4-166M-T7 with a spinning reel loaded with 10-lb. Power Pro braid, for small-fish inshore vertical jigging.

The Cara T7 is built on a graphite blank, has cork grips, Fuji ACS graphite reel seats, and Fuji Alconite Concept guides. The rod's finish is matte black, with glossy epoxy over the wraps.

The Cara Reaction rods in this series have a slower action, and should be checked out by vertical jiggers who are die-hard believers in the taut-line drop. They go for around $200. Patriotic Angler Bonus: Falcon is one of the few rods around that still holds the "Made in the USA" label.

The Falcon's a favorite for light-tackle jigging.

Shimano Trevala

Big-game jigging, anyone? If you want to target large fish by speed jigging, Shimano's Trevala and Trevala F rods—designed specifically for the Butterfly system—are the best I've found yet, period. Despite looking and feeling like rods intended for medium-sized inshore fish in the 10 to 20 pound class, like stripers and blues, these rod have an unreal amount of strength and can take on tunas and other high-power pelagics. They're also surprisingly inexpensive, at $150 to $200.

Trevalas, available in both spinning and conventional versions, have a limber tip that bends easily but tapers quickly into a stiffer mid-section, and then a stout lower section. It'll load and unload easily, with any reasonably sized jig. Thanks to the combination of light weight, strength, and action, it's a speed jigger's dream.

Shimano's marketing speak: the blank utilizes "TC4" construction, fusing a high-carbon butt section with a TC4 tip. The two together allow for high sensitivity without giving up strength, while producing an action that recovers its shape quickly. What the heck is TC4, anyway? The blank has an inner spiral layer of high modulus graphite, wrapped with two horizontal layers of fabrics. Then the blank is wrapped with another spiral pattern of high modulus graphite. The blank continues all the way through the grip for added strength.

The Trevala is amazingly potent for its size.

Grips are a closed-cell foam that is far firmer then what you'll find on most rods and won't work as a hook holder... as if you'd want to chew up the grips on this rod, anyway. The butts are exceptionally long, designed for tucking under your arm while speed jigging. Guides are Fuji SIC (silicon carbide).

Standing in the tackle shop, I'll bet dollars to doughnuts you hold a Trevala in you hand, and think "there's no way this rod can handle big tuna fish." Well, on my boat we've caught 'em well over 100-pounds using the 6'9" TFC-69ML, a rod which is rated to handle braid up to 50-pound test. Believe it – these rods will surprise the heck out of you!

Reels

Diamonds may be a girl's best friend, but guys like gold.

Now that you've got a rod all picked out, you'll need to put a reel on it. Make sure that when you shop, you have that rod with you — no matter how you hold a reel in your hands, you'll never get a realistic feeling for how the handle sits in your palm, how the weight balances on any given stick, or if it's easy to engage and disengage freespool with one hand. It's got to be mounted, and held the way you'll be fishing it.

When it comes to jigging, should you be looking at spinning or conventional gear? Spinning gear is a lot of fun to use and modern advancements have resulted in several models that can stand up to relatively big game. Add in the facts that with braid you eliminate the line twist problem and can load twice the amount of line onto spool that may have seemed half-sufficient with monofilament, and you have a winning combination. That doesn't mean you should set out to conquer giant tunas with spinning reels, but for most fish up to the 80 or possibly even into the 100-pound class, spinning gear is an option. Keep in mind that you will have less line capacity then a conventional rig of similar size and weight, and that you can't put as much pressure on fish when pumping the rod.

Some other anglers will opt for conventional gear, not only because of the ability to take on larger game but also because it enables them to control the drag settings more accurately during a fight. If, that is, they're using a lever drag reel. These will usually cost between $100 and $300 more then similar reels with star drags, but it's a worthwhile expense. It allows for one-handed drag adjustments which can be made secure in the knowledge that "X" clicks of the lever will tighten or loosen the drag up by exactly "Y" pounds of pressure. If you can afford the lever drag models, go for it.

Another consideration when looking at conventional reels is spool width. Yes, wider spools accommodate more line, but consider narrow spool reels before you buy. The drop in capacity gets you better balance on the rod — anglers used to extra wide-spool models know how they tend to force the rod to roll left then right in your hands as you crank them — and it also eliminates the need for level winding. (Just to put the thought to rest, no, you can't jig pelagics with a level-winder reel. The fast runs of bluewater fish will fry the worm gear.) With narrow spool models the line tends to lay itself back and forth without any assistance from the angler, freeing up your attention and your left thumb. If you have the financial ability to do so, it's worth going for the narrow spool even if it means jumping up a size class to get the line capacity you need.

Note that many jigging reels, even some designed for big game, don't come with lugs. If the reels you choose have no lugs there's no sense in using gimbaled butts, since you can't strap into a belt and harness anyway. You can add lugs to any reel, however, by picking up a "Get Strapped" bracket (about $25). These slide onto the bolts securing the clamp to the reel, between the rod and the reel seat. I have a set on a Shimano Trinidad TN30 rig (which doesn't come with lugs) and it works great.

This Penn Torque has lugs, but many jigging reels intended for big-game hunting do not.

Just how much line capacity is enough? Naturally, that depends on how and where you will fish. And, there are no hard and fast rules; this is fishing, and what works for one guy one day may simply not work for someone else, another day. But, here's a general rule of thumb: when fishing for fast-swimming pelagics or when jigging in very deep waters, if your line's pound-test capacity is equal to or more then the fish's weight, you'll want at least triple the depth of the water in line on your reel. That works out nicely since line capacity is measured in yards. An example: If you're going after 50-pound yellowfin with 50-pound test in 300' deep water, you'll want to have at the very least, 300 yards of line capacity. But remember, if you luck into that 100 pounder in this scenario, there's a good chance it'll spool you. The 100 pound possibility calls for twice as much line, or 600 yards of capacity.

Whether you like spinning or conventional gear, another feature jiggers must look for in a reel is speed, if you plan to apply speed jigging techniques. Yes, you need the whopping-big gears and you'll want a retrieve ratio of at least 5:1, with higher ratios generally being better. Remember, to get the speed jigging action you need to make that jig go fast – really fast. But don't allow speed alone to blind you to the other features of a reel. And by the same token, don't be lured by unnecessary features.

Dual-speeds are a great example of a feature you'll pay top dollar for, but will do virtually nothing for you. You'll find that you almost always use the reel in its high-speed gear, and when a fish sounds switching into low gear really doesn't help — if the fish is pulling hard enough to take drag it's going to take drag, regardless of reel gearing. And when you can pump the rod you can pump it, regardless of reel gearing. "Winching" the fish up effectively in low gear? I have yet to see it happen. Save the extra $200 or so, get the one speed reel, and you'll never regret it.

Construction quality, however, is something you should be willing to spend extra on. Look for brass gears, forged, machined aluminum frames and spools, and the use of multiple ball-bearings.

On conventional reels, the smoother and longer the spool spins when in freespool, the better. You can easily test this with or without line on the reel, while standing in a tackle shop, by simply spinning it and seeing how long it goes and how smoothly it does so. Next, engage the clicker and give it a few cranks. Some guys like 'em loud, others don't. And, how easy or difficult is it to put on the clicker in the first place? On some reels, thanks to poor button placement or difficulty moving it, it's a struggle each and every time. If the reel has a star drag, reach over and see if you can adjust it with one finger while your palm remains on the crank. If not, you'll be unable to effectively adjust drag while fighting a fish.

When shopping for spinning reels, there are some different items to remain on the lookout for. Even though line twist isn't a huge issue with braid you'll want to make sure your bail has a decent roller bearing, simply to reduce friction. Forget about finding one with a drag that's adjustable with any degree of certainty as to poundage during the fight; this is more or less impossible and remains a weakness of spinners. You should, however, look for a drag adjustment knob that clicks or passes over indents as it turns, so you can feel how many clicks you make as you turn it and at least have an idea of how much or how little you're adjusting it at any time. Most importantly, any spinning reel used for jigging must, must, must have a good infinite anti-reverse feature. If it's slamming back against itself each and every time you swing the rod, your reel will have a very short lifetime. Here are my favorites, again in alphabetical order.

Abu Garcia Soron STX 70

The Soron STX 70 is a spinning reel that's designed for life in the brine, with gears made from heavy-duty corrosion-resistant brass. The body, rotor, and bail arm are made of X-Craftic, a corrosion-resistant aluminum alloy. The use of this aluminum alloy also makes for a light weight reel, and the STX 10 comes in just a hair over 20 ounces. The gear ratio is 4.8:1, pretty darn slow for speed jigging but fine for other forms of jigging. These reels make life easier for braid anglers, because the "Superline" spools won't let braids spin around the spool, the way it does on some reels. That eliminates the need to back your braid with a shot of monofilament.

With a capacity of 300 yards of 20 pound braid, the STX 70 is perfect for medium-duty inshore jigging. The anti-reverse is infinite, and the front-adjusted drag clicks with every turn. Cost is another thing you'll like, with a price tag of about $150.

Penn Torque TRQ 300

The Torque TRQ 300, available for around $400 with a star drag and for about $200 more in a lever drag version, has an insanely fast 6.3:1 ratio. It also features an open, single-piece frame which makes level-winding easy and casting an option. You can pack over 400 yards of 80-pound braid onto this mini-beast, and crank down the drag until you can't hold on any longer.

I had a problem with the original disengaging pinion in my test reel, which broke after a few weeks of use and had to be replaced. But in all fairness Penn promptly fixed it under warranty, and it hasn't failed since. (Nor have I heard complaints from other anglers, about this model. If it were an endemic problem, I believe I would have heard more by now.) Otherwise it's held up well to the marine environment. I particularly like the fact that this reel has lugs, a feature many of the other reels designed for jigging and discussed in this section neglect. The best part of the Torque, however, is that it's simply comfortable to use. The balance, handle shape, and size of the reel just seem to blend well, and it's really a pleasure to have the Torque in your hands for all types of jigging.

The Torque gives you big game capability at a mid-range price point.

Shimano Torsa

The Torsa is a jigger's dream reel.

If you like fishing for big game with what passes for ultralight tackle in the open ocean, then you need to try out Shimano's Torsa 16N. Spooled up with 65 pound braid you'll be able to sock it to the tunas with 25 pounds of drag, no problem all day any day, while the spool's holding around 500 yards of line.

By virtue of the shape and size of the 16N's spool, line lays neatly down across it and level-winding isn't necessary at all. Meanwhile, the ratcheted lever drag is easily adjustable without even taking your hand off the crank; going in and out of freespool feels natural, and the lever and ratchet are beefy enough that they feel solid going in and out of gear — just like the metal-on-metal feel of shucking a shotgun. The Torsa also has awesome gearing with a 5.8:1 ratio and gears so massive they're 75-precent larger than those in a TLD. Each and every turn of the handle rips in almost four feet of line. I've been using one for several seasons now without any signs of failure or corrosion, period. To this day, the 16N remains my very favorite rig for speed jigging tunas, meat jigging in depths to 700' and vertical jigging over wrecks and reefs. 20, 30, and 40 class model Torsas are also available. One down-side: these suckers are expensive. Very expensive, to the tune of about $760. Yeah, I know: ouch! But if you can afford 'em, get 'em.

Shimano Torium 30

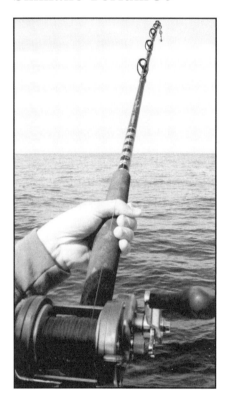

The Shimano Toruim is an excellent choice for people who have to live within a normal budget.

Want to get into the big-game speed jigging game without breaking the bank? Shimano's Torium is a relatively low-cost reel that has the speed, beef, and line capacity you need, yet costs less then the competition.

At 23.3 ounces, it's one of the lighter reels of this size and you can swing it all day without growing tired. Its 6.2:1 gear ratio is perfect for zipping jigs through the water column, and the star drag is positioned so you can adjust it with your thumb without taking your hand off the handle.

Sure, a lever drag would be even better, but that's a cost-boosting item that the Torium does well without. These reels have a diecast aluminum frame, a stamped aluminum side plate, and an aluminum spool. Also take note of the handle and crank, a part of many inexpensive reels that's woefully lacking. You'll find it comfortable to grip, and cranking up from 600' isn't nearly the chore it feels like with some gear.

Freespool is silky-smooth, and the drag is, too. Line capacity is sufficient for most situations, at 500 yards of 60 pound braid. There have been reports (I have not experienced this personally) of some anti-reverse failures with the Toriums due to pushing the envelope on drag settings and jig weights, but it should be noted that at this price point — the Torium costs just a hair over $200 — you're not going to find a reel that's impervious to heavy-hitting pelagics for extended periods of time. 20, 30, and 50 class models are also available.

Shimano Trinidad 20

The Trinidad is extrordinarliy tough - and expensive.

The Trinidad is much like the Torium but with a forged aluminum frame, stamped side plates, and chrome-plated screws. Essentially, it's beefed up and stronger inside and out. Otherwise it feels and performs similarly, and I've had a 20 (12 to 50 class models can be had) in my jigging arsenal for years. It's performed flawlessly despite a long history of saltwater dousings, screaming-drag runs, and living an otherwise hard life.

The gear ratio is a zippy 6.2:1, so the Trinidad is good for speed jigging as well as other forms of jigging. The 20 weighs in at 20 ounces, so swinging it all day long is no problem. Six ball bearings live inside the Trinidad, and the "super-stopper" prevents any kick-back when jigging.

One down-side to Trinidads: for star-drag reels, they are mighty expensive. Again, I've beat the heck out of one of these for many years to no ill effect and it's one of the best made star drag reels I've ever seen. But... a 20 goes for about $420, which is enough cash to get you several lever drag models. Time to pony up, big spender.

Shimano Saragosa

The Saragosa is a heavy-duty spinner designed for the salt, and the 1800 is the king of this hill. Rated to hold 380 yards of 20-pound test monofilament, squeezing on 400 yards of 60-pound braid is not a problem. And you can crank down that drag to take the kind of pressure such heavy test deserves, too. Shimano claims the drag can be torqued all the way to 44 pounds of drag; the reels I've used have been tuned to 25-pounds or so — enough to nearly yank my arms out of their sockets — and with some work I suppose they could be tightened down even more. It weighs in at a whopping 28.4 ounces, which is over

The Saragosa is a spinner that's capable of taking on bluewater pelagics.

three ounces more then the stand-by similarly-sized Penn 750 SS.

The Saragosa's anti-reverse is instant, so there's no slamming of metal on metal as you jig. Also took note of the handle shank, which is machined aluminum. On many spinners this is one spot where the manufacturer tries to save money, and if you stress the shank from side to side, it'll bend… until the day it breaks, of course. But this one's sturdier than the norm and won't give one bit when stressed.

The gear ratio is 4.9:1, the machined-aluminum spool is titanium-rimmed, and the Power Roller III line roller prevents heat build-up at the bail. Put these features together, and you have an offshore-capable reel you can cast and retrieve, without mass tangles. At $300 this is a pretty expensive spinner, but it does a job most spinning reels can't live up to.

Chapter 6: Jigging Tackle & Rigging – Lines, Leaders, and Jigs

Lines

This is 80-lb. Mono on the left, and 80-lb. Braid on the right. Note that the braid is visibly thinner, and the dime is raised higher sitting on the mono. You'll be able to get 40- to 50-percent more line on your spool using braid.

The reason jigging has really taken off as a multi-technique style of fishing has an awful lot to do with equipment advances. The rods we talked about earlier have improved actions and boosted strengths while they've shrunk in diameter and weight. The reels feature gears that have developed like they were injected with bovine growth hormone, and drags with capabilities that used to be available only in reels so dang big you had to sit down to use them. But the third piece of the jigging puzzle is every bit as important: braid line. Without it, the whole jigging thing would be a bust.

There are two attributes that make braid so imperative to jigging, both of which we've already touched on a bit. First, the no-stretch characteristic. Try jigging with mono in one hand and braid in the other, and you'll find that the braid-rigged line gets hit twice as often, because twice as much action is transferred from the rod to the lure. Actually, even if both were to get hit the exact same number of times you wouldn't know it anyway because you'll only feel half as many of those hits using the mono rig. When vertical jigging, especially, the sensitivity difference is amazing. I've tried deep dropping with mono in 800' of water, and you can hardly tell when a four pound weight has reached the bottom. But drop down the same rig with braid, and you can feel a six-inch rosy nipping gingerly at the bait. You can feel the weight stick in a mud bottom, and bounce on a hard bottom — it's truly an amazing difference.

Angler's Tip

When spooling up, you need braid to be extremely taunt. Otherwise when serious pressure is applied the line will cut into the spool, and create a bird's nest. Avoid this problem by dropping the spool into a bucket of water, then tensioning it with a cotton cloth as it's cranked onto the reel.

The no-stretch quality also boosts your hook-setting ability. Whether you're speed jigging, vertical jigging, or just jigging in incredibly deep water, you'll have the ability to set your hook with a short snap of the rod. No more multiple jabs, and wondering if you've gotten enough force down to that hook point. In fact, quite often while speed jigging and a fish strikes during the retrieve, or when vertical jigging and you go to sweep your rod tip up, you'll get a de-facto hook set simply because there's no slack and no stretch.

So, what's the second big advantage of braid, which makes many of these jigging styles possible? Lower diameter then mono of a comparable strength. That's why a reel that looks barely big enough to hold 300 yards of 50 pound test can suddenly hold 600 yards without giving up one iota of breaking strength. And this difference makes a reel that had barely enough line capacity to jig for sea bass in 150' of water suddenly capable of taking on tuna fish.

Like all other things on Planet Earth, braid also does have some down-sides endemic to its nature. So before anyone throws all their monofilament away and goes 100-percent braid, let's point out a few other factors: for certain types of fishing braid absolutely stinks. Chumming and chunking are the most significant examples. Not only can you feel the fish when using braid, they can feel you a whole lot better, too! Sink a bait in a chum slick on a braid rig and you'll discover that fish after fish spits your bait out in a fraction of a second, because they can immediately tell something is wrong. Live-baiting is another situation where mono has an advantage.

Another problem is the danger-factor associated with braid; anyone who's ever gotten it wrapped around a finger while a fish was on the other end of the line knows exactly what I'm talking about. This stuff is so hard to break and so thin that it cuts skin like a razor blade. Make the mistake of wrapping 100-pound braid on a nylon cleat, as I did once, and it'll saw right through the cleat itself. Breaking off when a jig is stuck in a wreck or reef can be nearly impossible, and in this situation if you try to apply too much pressure with a rod, there's a good chance you'll shatter it. Braid tangles are a real treat, too.

> **Captain's Tip**
>
> If your cleats are stainless — not nylon — you can use the cleat trick to temporarily hold your boat over a hotspot. Spool up a reel with 120 or 150 pound braid, and put a large treble hook on the end along with a few ounces of weight. When you get the boat over a select chunk of wreckage and you want to hold it there, use this rig to snag it. Cleat off the braid as tightly as possible, and in calm sea conditions this will hold you directly over the hotspot for several minutes (or until the first big wave comes along, and breaks the line). Remember: don't do it with nylon or plastic cleats...

So don't get the wrong idea — braid isn't the end-all, be-all fishing line and it does have its own share of problems. But when it comes to jigging of any form it does beat mono, resoundingly and hands-down.

Which specific types of braid are best? This is another argument which hinges on personal preference. Some guys love Fireline, others swear by Power Pro. Some love Gorilla Braid, others feel Magibraid is best. Frankly, I've used 'em all and can't tell a whole heck of a lot of difference from one brand to the other. All are made with either Spectra or Dyneema. Spectra, made by Honeywell, is a polyethylene fiber which (Honeywell claims) is pound for pound 15 times stronger then steel. Dyneema, invented by a company called DSM in the Netherlands, is a very similar product. In fact, in the industry they're often called "sister" lines, and both are made via the gel-spun polyethylene process. These braids aren't to be confused with "fused" lines, which essentially are heated to fuse some of the fibers together. This produces a strong and abrasion-resistant line, but one that's also stiff, troublesome when slack, and sometimes difficult to knot. (Though all superlines are to some degree — more on that later.) Some lines claim to be rounder then others, and hence cast or cut the water better. Some others claim to be more or less supple.

Warning: incredibly bad pun to follow

The bottom line? (Ahem.) If you like one more then another by all means stay partial to it, but don't knock yourself out trying to get all of one kind of braid or another, because they are extremely similar. Personally I've taken a real liking to Power Pro, and I can't even place my finger on exactly why that is. It does seem a bit more malleable then most lines and maybe it knots better, but it also costs a heck of a lot more then some others... go figure.

Choosing line test for your main line is another tough call. As a starting point, make sure the line's breaking strength at least approximately fits into the rated class of the rod and reel you're spooling it on. That said, here's a rule-of-thumb guide (for anglers who enjoy sporting-quality fights on relatively light tackle; die-hard meat-anglers will want to up the ante a bit) to appropriate classes for different sized fish:

Tunas/pelagics over 100 pounds	— 80 to 120 pound braid
Tunas/pelagics under 100 pounds	— 50 to 80 pound braid
Inshore species 50 to 100 pounds	— 30 to 50 pound braid
Inshore species under 50 pounds	— 10 to 50 pound braid

Now, let's get back that knotting issue. When attaching a lure, swivel, or other terminal tackle to braid the old stand-by improved clinch (Fisherman's) knot won't cut it, because of the line's slippery nature. Tie one, even with extra twists, and it's likely to pull out. Instead, go with the Palomar knot. This one's very easy to tie and once you're used to it, a Palomar becomes even faster then a Fisherman's. Here's how it goes:

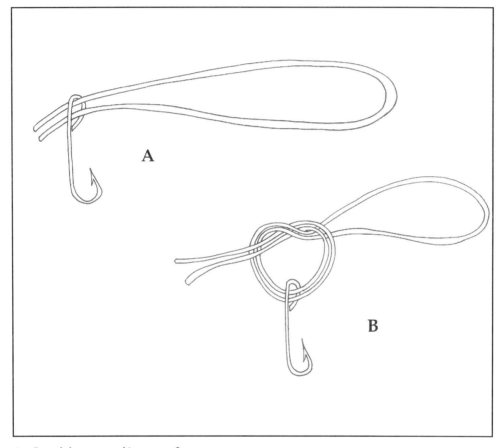

A. Double your line to form a loop in the end, and push it through the eye of your hook, lure, or swivel.

B. Tie an overhand knot in the doubled line.

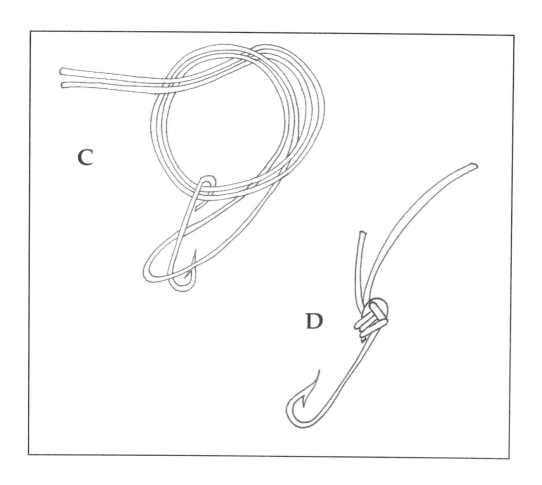

C. Slide the hook, lure or swivel back through the loop in the end of the line.

D. Release the loop, and pull the doubled main line against the hook, lure or swivel, drawing the knot tight. Cut off the excess.

Leaders

For many forms of jigging, you'll want to attach a leader to your line. Most people assume leaders are necessary to reduce visibility, prevent line chaff and give you some extra beef at the end of the fight. All good reasons to buy that fluorocarbon, though the visibility factor is over-played in my opinion, and appropriately sized braid has plenty of beef. But an often overlooked reason is adding some stretch into the equation, for the end game. When a big fish is up close to the boat and it surges, if there isn't some give to the line then there's a good chance the hook will pop free or something will break — so don't go leader-free when you're hunting big game. That said, for smaller fish it usually does no harm to tie directly to your main line.

Connecting your leader to your main line requires the use of different knots, either the Spider Hitch or the Bimini Twist. These knots are used to put a loop into the end of your line (or create a section of double line.) Which one's best? My personal preference is the Spider hitch — also known as a Hillbilly Bimini — for several reasons. First off, it's a lot faster and easier to tie one. A Bimini Twist takes far longer, and involves a lot more fancy steps and twists. Because of this, people get them wrong fairly often. I've watched seasoned anglers tie a Bimini, then watch (and just about cry) when it unraveled on the first decent fish of the day. In a nutshell, that complexity makes it easy to mess up. When tied correctly, yes, a Bimini will hold well in braid. But, why even consider doing it in the first place? A good, solid Spider Hitch can be done a heck of a lot faster and doesn't break any easier. (Admittedly, some sharpies will argue a Bimini has a few percentage points of advantage when it comes to breaking strength. But in my experience, it's certainly not enough to ever make a noticeable difference. With a good Spider Hitch in the line, 99 times out of 100 something other then the knot will break first.) So, I see no advantage to doing the complex knot instead of the simple knot.

Here's how to tie a Spider Hitch:

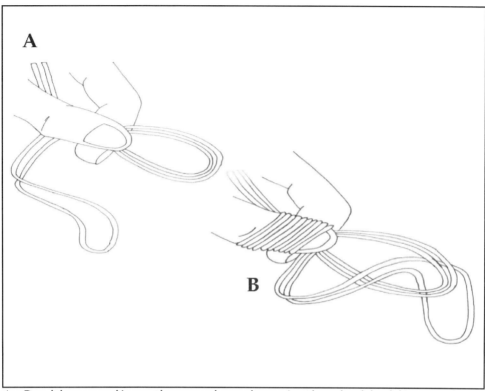

A. Double your line, then make a loop in the doubled line and pinch it between your thumb and forefinger.

B. Wrap the line around the end of your thumb, and the loop where it's pinched under your thumb, five times. Then push the end of the doubled line through the loop.

C. Pull the end of the line, and the loops will pull off of your thumb one by one. When they're all off, pull the knot tight and trim off any excess.

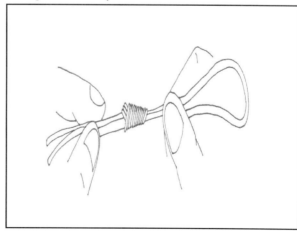

Pre-tied fluorocarbon leaders terminate in a loop, which makes life easy — after you've made the loop in the end of your main line with a Spider Hitch, simply do a loop-to-loop connection to attach the two. (No diagram necessary, this is a piece of cake – push the loop at the end of your leader through the loop in the end of your main line, pass the tag end of your leader through it's loop, and pull it tight.) Do not, however, tie a braid end directly to the loop in the fluorocarbon, as the single line wrapping the mono tends to cut into it when under strain; the loop-to-loop distributes the stress better and prevents this problem.

What leader is the best? First off, fluorocarbon has a refractive index closer to that of water then mono does, making it nearly invisible and thus clearly superior to nylon monofilament as a leader material. (Did you catch the lousy pun in that sentence? If not, there is clearly something wrong with you.) An example: A few seasons back while trawler-chunking, we pulled an entire school of bluefin tuna off of a scalloper and held it at our boat for the entire morning. This gave us a unique opportunity to try some comparative tests, and one we did was on leaders. (Note: this was in gin-clear blue-ish water, about 45 miles off the coast.) We started with 120-pound fluoro leaders and watched the fish swim right up to the bait, then stop and turn away. (As they ate un-hooked chunks slowly but without hesitation; in this situation the fish were acting rather lazy, and were taking their time about eating.) Then we continually dropped leader size by 10-pound test increments, until the fish started striking — which was at 40-pound test. Then we tied on some mono leaders. The fish refused them one after another, with a few of the less-cautious fish striking 30-pound test but most avoiding even this. The difference was quite obvious, and I've stuck purely with fluorocarbon as a leader material whenever fishing for leader-shy fish, ever since.

This isn't to say there's no room on the boat for mono leaders. In fact, when fishing inshore in dirtier water for species like bluefish, stripers, and weakfish, I'm not sure it makes a darn bit of difference. But if tunas are your target, buy the good stuff.

One problem with fluorocarbon: it's pretty stiff, and it doesn't knot as easily as mono. As a result, you'll be better off by crimping all connections that you make in any leader over 60-pound test. Luckily, you can buy pre-tied wind-on leaders in just about every imaginable size and brand. As long as you get a reputable, known brand, most of the leaders do seem to be about the same quality. P-Line, Yo-Zuri, Seaguar, and Shimano are all good examples. Which of those sizes should you choose? Here's a rule-of-thumb guide to use as a starting point, for anglers who enjoy sporting fights on relatively light tackle.

Tunas/pelagics over 100 pounds	—	**120 to 160 pound test**
Tunas/pelagics under 100 pounds	—	**60 to 120 pound test**
Inshore species 50 to 100 pounds	—	**30 to 80 pound test**
Inshore species under 50 pounds	—	**20 to 60 pound test**

Yup, there's quite a huge range here. That's because you'll have to judge leader size based on the reaction of the fish. The rule is to start on the heavy side, and drop down as necessary. If you're speed jigging for bluefin in the 80 pound class, for example, start off with 120 leaders and if you don't get hit fairly quickly, drop one or two of your rigs down to 100. Still no hits? Try 80, then 60. In this scenario you can usually get away with a relatively heavy leader as compared to bait fishing, because most of the time speed jigging will create a reaction strike that triggers a quick gut response from the fish. They won't be taking time to eyeball it but will be slashing at the bait, so leader size is less imperative. Still you'll still have days when switching to lighter leaders is necessary. The good news? A loop-to-loop connection makes for very fast and easy leader changes. Don't try to pull that braid's loop apart, though. A few cranks with a hefty jig is all it takes to cinch it down tight and you'll spend more time fighting the loop then you will by cutting the braid a quarter inch up, and pulling it off. Then, cut off the remainder of the old loop and tie a new Spider Hitch in the end.

You can also buy your fluorocarbon in bulk and tie wind-ons yourself, either by using a "direct drive" low-profile swivel that's small enough to fit through your guides to make the braid to leader connection, by tying a Spider Hitch in the leader, or by crimping to create a loop on one end. All of these methods have up and down sides. I don't like using the swivels for a number of reasons: they can crack or chip guide liners; often they have sharp edges and force abrupt bends in the line which weakens it; and they never seem to sit straight with a Palomar knot attaching them. So I don't use 'em. I do know some real pros who do, though.

Tying a Spider Hitch works great with leaders of 60 pound test and down. With 80 it's very difficult to get a Spider Hitch to cinch down properly, and with anything thicker it's impossible. Besides, half the time you'll end up with a knot so thick it won't go through the guides properly, anyway.

What about crimping in a loop? Again, by running hard-edged metal through your guides over and over again as large fish put a huge amount of pressure on the line, eventually, that little piece of metal is going to crack or chip a line guide. Or worse, pass across your finger as you're level-winding — ouch! These problems are why, as a general rule of thumb most anglers will be better served by buying pre-tied wind-on leaders.

Jigs

Choices, choices, choices! When you go jig shopping you'll discover a zillion and one different color patterns, shapes, sizes, and qualities. First off, get a dedicated jig bag with padded slots. Leave your heavy jigs banging around in a plastic tackle box and the paint will chip off on your first two-hour offshore run. Next, get plenty of hooks, split and solid rings, because many modern jigs come un-rigged. Sizing up these items is tough; despite a heck of a lot of research into the subject I've found there is no authoritative guide to matching them up, mostly because you can find different sources of literature from the ***very same manufacturer*** which contradict each other. So this is yet another time where I'll have to remind people that what you read on these pages is what I've found to be effective; there is no hard and fast "right" or "wrong" and you may have your own opinion that differs from mine. I encourage experimentation — and for folks to e-mail their results to me!

Jig (grams)	Split Ring	Solid Ring	Hook Size
55 and under	#4 - #5	#4 - #5	1/0
55 to 120	#5 - #7	#6.5	2/0 - 4/0
120 to 200	#7 - #9	#7.5	5/0 - 7/0
200 to 400	#9 - #10	#7.5 - #9	7/0 - 9/0
400+	#10	#9	8/0+

Table Specs:
- One ounce = 28.35 grams.
- All split and solid ring sizes are based on Owner Hyper Wire.
- Hook size is based on Owner Dancing Stinger. (*Hook size varies from manufacturer to manufacturer. Hooks are available on shorter and longer leaders, IMHO shorter is better, period.*)

When it comes to actually rigging these jigs, again, different sources differ on the "best" method. Specific methods that better match a specific type of jigging are covered in the other chapters of this book, but generally, most people rig up with a single or double hook at the top of the jig, and no hook on the bottom.

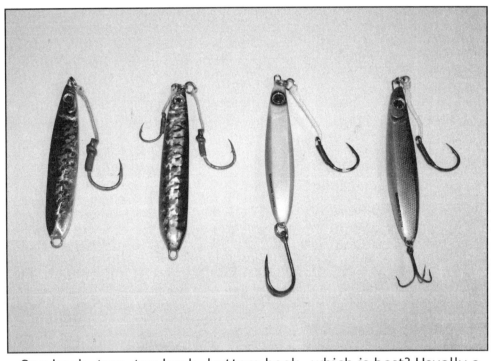

One hook, two, top hook, bottom hook...which is best? Usually a single/top (far left) is all you want—but in certain situations this will change, as noted later in this chapter.

Which is better, one hook or two? One good source at Shimano told me two was the way to go, another said it made little to no difference. After experimenting with a single hook, a pair of identical hooks, and paired hooks of differing sizes and leader lengths, I've come to the conclusion that it makes little to no difference, and thus rig up with a single top hook the majority of the time. But...

As mentioned earlier, I've come to believe it's advantageous in some vertical jigging, combination vertical/speed jigging scenarios, and when meat jigging, to add a stout treble to the bottom of the jig. Specifically, this will help when you're experiencing a lot of pull-offs (and are not jigging on hard structure that's easily snagged; add a treble in this situation and you'll lose a lot more tackle). Speed jigging for bluefin on the inshore lumps, where several vertical jigging motions are in order before you give a speed retrieve, is a perfect example. (We'll get a bit more in-depth on this specific topic later.)

If you opt for a two-hook rigging style, make sure the two leaders are cinched down on opposite sides of your solid ring so they don't tangle. And whether you're rigging singles, doubles, or whatever, look out for the hook to double back and catch around the thinner section of the jig. In some cases the jig, hook, and hook leader are sized just right so that the hook's point wraps around the jig and the barb grabs the other side of it. Locked down like this, you can get hit after hit after hit without ever having a hook up. There's no common rule as to hook size and jig size that will explain and solve this problem, because of differing shapes and lengths that vary as you go from manufacturer to manufacturer. To prevent this you'll just have

Warning: *Stay away from thin crimped wire hook leaders on large jigs used for fish over 60 or 80 pounds, which don't have the pound-test of the leader marked on the packaging. While the wire prevents tangles and keeps the hook from wrapping the jig, this stuff isn't as strong as it looks. I've seen it break on gamefish in the 70 to 80 pound range several times, and now reserve its use for inshore fish.*

to keep an eye out for the issue and change hooks and/or jigs as necessary.

Whatever hook arrangement you're using, the hook should be attached by running the leader through the solid ring, then push the loop over the hook and pull it tight. Next, attach a split ring to the solid ring. Then your leader is tied or crimped, depending on side, to the solid ring.

Most sources then tell you to attach your leader to the solid ring. Some experienced jiggers, however, feel that attaching your main line to the solid ring invites break-offs, because these rings have a fairly hard edge. I have to agree that knots tied onto the rings look like they are under a lot of stress because of this. However, I've never reeled in a line with the broken knot at the end, nor one broken beyond the crimp. And if you tie onto the split ring instead of the solid, your knot could get nicked by the sharp edges of steel where it wraps around. For these reasons, I still attach to the solid ring... except when I don't. When going after large pelagics with light gear you need each and every connection working at 110-percent, and one option which I've found useful when targeting them is to tie or crimp a small ball-bearing swivel directly to the main line, then attach it to the jig via the split ring. This eliminates the hard edge issues, and it's just as easy to constantly swap out jigs. Is it absolutely necessary to add in that swivel? No, and it does introduce another point of potential failure. But it makes me feel a lot more confident in the overall rigging then just attaching to the solid ring.

Speaking of potential points of failure: note that there's no snap swivel involved in this rigging. Been there, done that. The snap is too close to where the fish strike near the head of the lure, and they'll actually open up snap swivels now and again when they chomp down on your jig. It sounds crazy, but I had it happen several times before I completely abandoned the use of snap swivels while jigging.

With your line and hook(s) attached to the rings, you're ready to leave the dock — don't put on a jig, just yet. One of the nice things about this rigging style is that you can slip a jig's eye onto the split ring in a matter of seconds. Not only will this allow for instant jig changes, providing you with the ability to switch color, shape, or size on a whim, it also allows you to cruise with little to no weight on the end of your line. Note: larger split rings require the use of split ring pliers designed specifically for this purpose.

If you've ever ducked (or worse yet failed to duck) a 10-ounce jig sling-shotting around the end of a rod while the boat's running through rough seas, then you know how advantageous it is to cruise with no jig on your line. Still, you want one on there so that your rig is always ready to fish with. A good option is to purchase "cocoons," small neoprene wraps with Velcro tabs on the edges, which cinch the jig down tight against your rod or grip. They work well, and I use these when cruising from spot to spot.

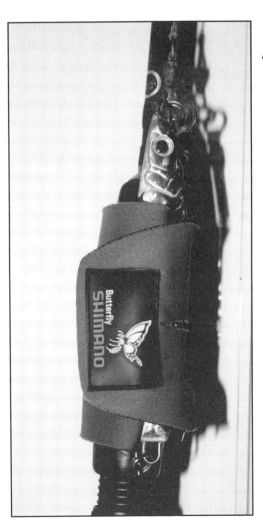

Cocoons, neoprene wraps with Velcro ends, work well for holding your jigs in place while cruising from spot to spot. Note the ball-bearing swivel connecting the line to the split ring.

Of course, before you rig a jig, you'll have to choose one from the tackle shop racks. There are gazillians of jigs out there, of all different styles, shapes, and colors, so this can be a tough choice. For specific species in specific situations, there are certain jigs that are clearly superior to others. These will be covered on a case-by-case basis, in the chapters covering those fish. In every fishing situation, however, you'll have to deal with three main choices: color, size, and shape.

All of these three factors are incredibly important to bear in mind when choosing a jig, because they work together to determine the jig's visibility, action, and appeal. But size is going to have the be ranked number one in importance, simply because the weight of a jig is the number-one determining factor is how and where you can use it. If you can't get deep enough to tempt the fish (or conversely, if your jig remains underneath them at all times) you're not going to catch much.

Choosing the right jig is tough, thanks to essentially endless choices.

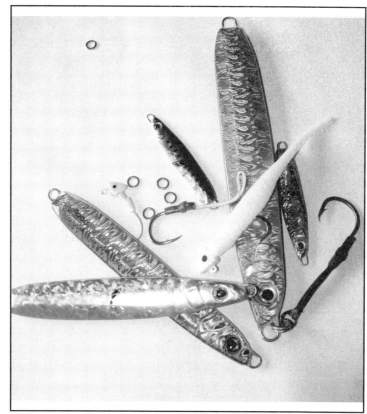

The general rule of thumb: use the minimum amount of weight necessary to reach the depth of the fish and stay there. An exception: Speed jiggers need only get beneath the fish, and don't have to worry so much about staying at that specific depth. The lighter your jig is the less chance its weight slinging back and forth will help pop a hook free, or work open a hole in the fish's jaw. Lighter jigs are also less tiring to use, and quite often you can get a better action out of them at a lower speed of travel. But don't err or the side of lightness. When vertical jigging right on bottom, for example, you'll need to maintain contact with the bottom on the down-swing. If the current or wind is moving the boat along at a speedy clip and your jig's too light, you'll need to constantly let out line to do so. That takes time, means you'll have a longer fight to get the fish up to the boat, and boosts the chances of tangling other angler's lines. Note that when multiple anglers are dropping at the same time, the person with the lighter jig should always be positioned in the down-current position in the cockpit. They should also drop a second or two before anyone else, so their jig gets pulled away from the boat first, to minimize tangling.

How much weight is the right amount? Again, this will change in every situation. Current strength, wind speed, and other factors will constantly change weight requirements. But as a general rule of thumb you'll usually want two to four ounces in water under 50' deep; four to eight in waters down to 100' or so; six to 10 in water to 200' deep; and 10 to 20 in waters to 300' or 400'. Beyond that, go for the heaviest you've got. On a calm day in 700' of water you can hit bottom with a 12-ounce jig, for instance, but it'll take three or four minutes to get there, and as soon as a breeze kicks up you'll lose touch unless you constantly let out line. For these deep-drops, two pound jigs are not out of line.

One more thing to keep in mind, when choosing size: matching the hatch. Shape plays a role here too, but if the predators are feeding on schools of five-inch sand eels, that 10" long 12 ounce jig might just get ignored. You'll want to drop down a relatively small jig even though it may be tougher to reach bottom, because that's what will generate the hits. Plus, smaller jigs are often more or less inhaled by large fish, eliminating pulled hooks and missed strikes. In each and every situation you're fishing in you'll have to take all of these considerations into account, and then make a judgment call—that's what being a good angler is all about.

Your next consideration is color. From walking through a well-stocked tackle shop you'd think you need 100 different colors and patterns to catch a sardine. In fact, a few solid stand-bys catch the vast majority of the fish. Commonly, you'll want to match your jig's color to the color of the water. In greenish water, look to chartreuse or lime. In blue water try blues and blue/purple patterns. In turbid, brownish water, gold is often a good bet.

A few cases that have to be mentioned in specific: pink/silver is an absolute killer for bluefin tunas on the inshore lumps of the mid Atlantic, when they're feeding on sand eels. Mackerel/silver is another one that draws a lot of hits. When deepwater jigging for golden tilefish, the chartreuse/white which glows and squid patterns earn top honors. And stripers often seem to like chartreuse or blue/silver combos the most.

Shape is the final determining factor in jig choice. Shimano alone has three distinct Butterfly models, the regular, flat-sided, and long varieties. Regulars are intended for speed-jigging (though they also work well for vertical jigging or yo-yoing,) and they give a walk-the-dog sort of motion as they go through the water. Flat-sided Butterflies have a slightly more erratic motion, but give essentially the same type of back and forth action. Personally I have yet to find a situation in which one of these styles didn't work and the other did, so I use 'em both. Not so for the Long style. These sink much more slowly, have a less erratic action, and are designed for speed jigging through the upper section of the water column. Shimano says they're for use in 150' or less, for fish including yellowtail, kingfish, and tunas. Maybe you'll find them great for these purposes but I haven't found a single situation yet in which I liked them more then flats or regulars, so I don't stock up on these.

A few more notes on the Butterflies in specific: these jigs do tend to have a faster, more erratic action then some of the competitors for speed jigging and yo-yoing. One experiment will allow you to prove it to you for yourself and at the same time, compare jig actions of different manufacturers head-to-head: with your boat in gear drop one over the side and tow it at two or three knots. Drop a competitor's jig of the same size into the water, and slowly increase speed. Watch those jigs — you'll discover that some "speed" jigs don't so much as flutter, while some others start to flutter only as you increase speed to seven or eight knots. And even when speed jigging, you'll rarely if ever achieve these rates of speed. How do I know...?

Shimano Butterfly jigs, from left to right: Long, Butterfly, and Flat.

While doing research for an article in *Boating* magazine, we once measured out distances and timed the retrieve of a casting plug on several different reels. Some were spinning, others conventional. Some were high speed, some not. The idea was to figure out the exact speed our lures were traveling at when retrieved. To make a long story short, we had to really struggle to get a lure up to six knots. In most cases with average reels, cranking as fast as possible we'd barely break five. Hard to believe? Yeah, I thought so, too. But remember the Torsa's comparatively super-fast 8 feet per second speed jigging retrieve? That's 480 feet per minute and there are 5,280 feet in a mile, so you're moving that jig at a rate of one mile every 11 minutes. Do the math — that's only 5.45 miles per hour. Only the reels with the greatest ratios and jiggers with the most ambition are going to get those lures traveling at a relatively high rate of speed. In other words, you need to use a jig that attains the motion you're looking for while traveling through the water between four and six miles per hour.

Of course, lures used for other forms of jigging don't necessarily have to be designed to give that darting action. Meat jiggers won't need to worry much at all about this factor since the action is slow and doesn't depend on an erratic motion of the jig to produce strikes. And vertical jiggers will find that virtually all jigs provide some level of fish-tempting action on the drop. Even those that fall more or less flatly will generate strikes, as they look to the predators like an injured, sinking fish.

What about other specific brands of jigs? There are several out there which you'll want to know about. Williamson is one brand that has appeared in tackle shops across the nation. Their Benthos model speed jigs share the Butterfly Long's basic shape and as you may guess, these aren't my favorites. Same goes for the Williamson's Abyss jigs, though they're weighted more on the back end then the front and do have a better sink and action. The Vortex are stubbier and sink nicely, have a good action for vertical and speed jigging, and are also fine for meat jigging if it's shallow and calm enough to use their comparatively smaller sizes. The nicest thing about Williamsons is that they have plenty of flash and they cost significantly less then many other jigs, sometimes half as much as a comparable Butterfly. They also come pre-rigged, which is both a blessing and a curse: you don't have to bother with rigging them up and buying additional parts and pieces, but you don't get to choose which size and type of hook you'll be using (at least not at the start; you can swap 'em out after the purchase).

Jerkthatjig jigs come in a wide, wide variety of shapes and sizes, including some spectacularly bizarre forms. The most unique model is the Clear Eyes, which has an open slot molded into the center of the jig. Mini cyalume glow-sticks clip into the slot, turning your jig into a lighted lure for night fishing or deep-dropping where the sun don't shine. I've found that the cyalume stick stays put, even when you whip your rod tip up at maximum velocity for hours at a time. The Red Eye is another bizarre and unusual jig, which looks like a pair of jigs molded together in the middle. The double-ended shape gives it a dancing motion that makes reef fish in particular snap at 'em when vertical jigging.

Jerkthatjig has some unusual offerings, like the Red Eye (left) and the Clear Eye (right).

Their speed jig models have a decent amount of action and are effective for speed jigging, yo-yoing and vertical jigging. But meat jiggers or deep-water jiggers looking for maximum weight will be particularly interested in this brand, because they offer some extraordinarily large models which range from 300 to 750 grams (10 to 26 ounces) in a multitude of color patterns. You like fishing for grouper and golden tilefish in water so deep, there's barely any light? These jigs also have a strip of glow paint running down the edges, to make them visible no matter how dark it gets. In 1,000' of water they'll hit bottom in just over three minutes, cutting the deep-drop dropping time by half in many cases. For meat-jigging at the edge of the Continental shelf in particular, these are a top pick.

Jerkthatjigs come with the hardware already installed, and

The bazooka of jigs, Jerkthatjigs mega-moster 750 gram model is ideal for deep-drop meat jigging.

the hook leader is copper-fiber Dacron coated with heat-shrink tubing. That makes them more or less impervious to toothy fish like kings and wahoo. These hooks are nice and sharp and well-sized for the jigs, but I have had them break on two occasions. I inquired about this with the principals at Jerkthatjig, and they said they had heard of no other instances in which this happened. Since I use these jigs quite a bit, I'm inclined to think I simply had a few hooks from a bad batch.

Megabait and Braid Slammers are two more brands that should have a place in your tacklebox. Neither gives a particularly great action for speed jigging, but both have incredibly flashy colorful finishes and are excellent for vertical jigging. Note, however, that these brands come pre-rigged with aft treble hooks — fine for jigging where there aren't many snags, but less then ideal for wreck or reef fishing.

A Braid jigging spoon.

Hopkins hammered-metal style jigs are a classic, and have been around forever. Like the Megabaits and Slammers they are rigged with a treble on the end and are best reserved for vertical jigging. One unique feature Hopkins offers is that they can be purchased with colored feathers dressing the hook.

A hammered-metal Hopkins.

There will be days that a Hopkins with yellow feathering is tops, particularly when jigging for schooled weakfish on shoals and bars. Added bonus: since they're hammered metal, a Hopkins never loses that shiny finish no matter how many rocks they bounce off of or how many times bluefish rake their teeth across the jig.

Luhr Jensen's Crippled Herring is another old classic that works when vertical jigging. These can be bought with single hooks on the bottom end, as opposed to trebles. Like a Hopkins they have a hammered-metal finish, but these also have color added in many different available patterns. Their action isn't my favorite, though.

Marias are another unique jig, and the only jigging "spoon" you'll want to consider that's not made of metal. These have a clear, soft, rubberized finish, which encases strips of flashy metallic foil and lead. Marias are tough to find sometimes (try to buy them on the web and you're more likely to find prices listed in yen then in dollars) but it's worth the effort. Surprisingly they sink very, very fast with far less weight then you'd expect, which makes them wonderful for light tackle anglers jigging for stripers, weakfish, fluke and the like. In fact, you can easily use a three inch, once ounce Maria on a light action spinning rod spooled with 12 pound test braid, and get the same bait size and sink rate as you would with most three ounce metal spoons. These wobble a bit when moved quickly through the water, but aren't tops for swimming action and have aft rigged trebles, so they should be more or less reserved for vertical jigging.

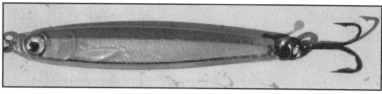

Marias are unique, and sink surprisingly fast for their weight.

What about wobbling spoons like Tonys, Acmes, Clarkes, and Crippled Alwives? These are intended for trolling, and they don't work well for jiggers at all. Of course, there are a million varieties of diamond jigs, hammered spoons, and other more traditional lures in all kinds of shapes and sizes. Naturally it wouldn't be possible to examine all in this book; generally speaking, most of the other brands and shapes are designed for traditional vertical jigging, and may or may not produce depending on many factors. And, there are also plenty of other styles of lures out there that can be jigged. Can be — but not necessarily should be. Most aren't designed for this type of fishing, and you won't maximize your catch using them. One exception: jig heads dressed with soft plastic tails. Many anglers use these exclusively for cast-and-retrieve fishing, but in many cases these types of jigs will work extremely well for vertical jigging. Usually, this will be inshore or in bays, where smaller gamefish like fluke, stripers, or weakfish are present and feeding on relatively small baits. In these cases, jigging with soft plastic tails will often be the top-producing technique.

Which tails to use? Wow — that could be a topic for another whole book! There are so many brands and styles it's nearly impossible to cover them all, but when you hit the bottom line, the most effective color, tail style, and size will vary in the same ways as other jigs. Most of the time, however, baits with added scents (especially Powerboats and GULP!s) will out-shine those without. My personal favorite go-to bait for general plastic jigging is a 5" chartreuse GULP! Jerk Shad. One GULP! down-side: these things are expensive. A pack of five tails goes for about seven bucks, so it's pretty painful when these things get chewed up by undersized fish, blues, or lots of use. Wait -

Soft plastics, like the Mister Twister Exude seen here on Fishing Buddy Mollie's line, work extremely well for vertical jigging inshore, and on bays.

there's one other thing you need to know about GULP! Never, ever allow it to dry out on your jig head. This stuff becomes hard as a rock, and is nearly impossible to cut away from the hook even with a sharp knife. If you forget and one solidifies, it can be re-hydrated by soaking it in a bucket for a few hours.

Another good scented plastic tail to consider is the Mister Twister Exude, and Fin-S or BKD's are good baits that come in handy when you don't believe the added attraction of scent is needed.

So far as the physical appearance of the tail goes, long, slender plastics work much better then deep-bodied baits with paddle tails on the end, when it comes to jigging. (Traditionally these paddle tail baits were identified as "Shad Body" or "Sassy Shad" but in the past few years manufacturers have taken to printing "shad" on the package of anything fish-shaped. Just remember to look for the deep body, as opposed to a long, slender one.) In fact, those baits are virtually worthless for vertical jigging – reserve their water-time for casting and retrieving, only. Twister tails can go either way, but experience will prove that these tails are also best utilized while casting.

One other important factor to consider, when jigging with plastics: the presence of toothy fish, like bluefish, Spanish mackerel, and kingfish. When these guys are around, you'll get "tailed" and reel up half your lure just as often as you'll hook fish. If you're using an expensive bait like those GULPS! This can be pretty aggravating. Now's the time to reach for your packet of Zman StreakZ. At four bucks a five-pack they're downright cheap, the tails have a great action, and most importantly, they can take a dozen or so hits from toothy fish before ripping or tearing. (Chomp down on one yourself, and you'll discover the plastic rolls out from under your teeth before any cutting can get done.

When shopping for speed jigs you may note that some manufacturers boast about finish quality and ruggedness, hardware quality, and longevity of the jig itself. In all cases except hammered metal jigs, the finish will get slightly chipped with time as fish slap them and they bounce off rocks or wreckage. The rubberized finish of Maria jigs won't "chip," of course, but it does eventually grow dull with age. Is one particular brand's finish "better" then another? Does one or the other have more longevity? If so, it's awful hard to tell. In most cases your jigs will need replacement because they've been snagged and broken off or bitten off by fish, not because they wore out. Two exceptions: falling tackleboxes, unsecured jigs bouncing around in a box, or other tackle disasters can lead to bent jigs; and of course, the hooks do rust out and need regular replacement.

Chapter 7: Behind the Scenes - The Butterfly System

® Shimano, photo courtesy of Shimano

Legalish Sounding Disclosure Comment:
This book and the contents of this chapter are not connected in any way with Shimano, and shouldn't be construed as "official" or "authorized by" Shimano. Nor am I personally connected to Shimano in any official or unofficial capacity. This is all my opinion and experience, period. Shimano did give me permission to use several photos in this chapter, and that's the extent of our relationship.

A huge portion of the credit for starting the current jigging craze goes to Shimano, without any doubt, thanks to the incredible success of the Butterfly system. Speed jigging originally took off in Japan, where anglers were targeting heavily-pressured bluefin in 500' of water. Thanks to all the pressure the fish had taken to holding deep and staying there, and anglers needed a way to present lures from the bottom up in a manner that would cause a reaction strike. (Sound familiar? Bluefin at the Hambone have dozens of boats trolling over their heads day after day, driving them down from the surface. Is it just a coincidence that the butterflies work so well here? Doubt it.) But according to several sources the technique that started it all was really yo-yoing, which progressed into speed jigging. The enabler was braid, first and foremost — with this new super-strong line it was possible to load up vast lengths of line, and since it didn't stretch jiggers could effectively impart action to their lures from hundreds of feet away.

Shimano picked up on the phenomenon early, and set about designing jigs that had asymmetrical 3-D shapes and differing weight distributions, which would generate the walk-the-dog motion as they traveled through the water at attainable rates of speed. Once this was accomplished rods and reels were developed to enhance the action and the angler's comfort level, allowed the technique to be refined and perfected to the point that it was recognizably different from yo-yoing.

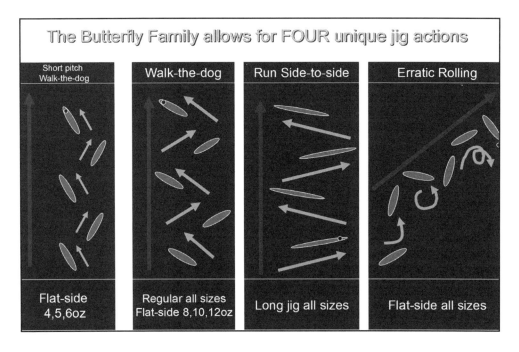

Illustration courtesy of Shimano.

What about the Butterfly technique itself? The one described in the section on speed jigging more or less follows the Butterfly structure — so you're already familiar with it. Here's one of Shimano's illustrations showing "their" motion for speed jigging with spinning gear:

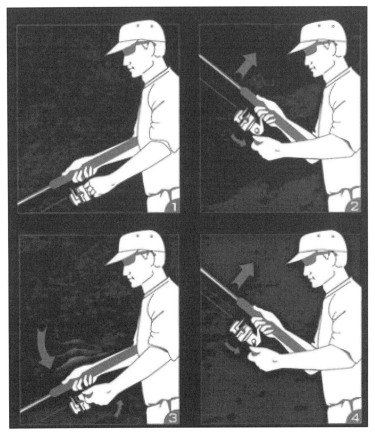

Illustration courtesy of Shimano.

As you can see, there's nothing startling about this. So, why should you care specifically about the Butterfly system? Because this is the only one that focuses solely on the speed jigging concept through each and every piece of tackle, right onto the technique. The reel, the rod, the line, the leader, and the lure are all designed and tweaked down to the last detail to make the ultimate combination for this one specific variety of fishing. And Shimano did the field work necessary to take the Butterfly system to its refined level, by testing the gear many times in multiple locations on multiple species of fish. Net result? If you go with an all-Shimano rig, there's no mixing and matching required. You don't have to get a reel from one manufacturer, a rod from another, and a jig from whoever, and then see if they all work well together. You at least will know you have the gear in-hand to accomplish your mission. The technique part of the equation, of course, can't be bought.

Speaking of rigs: as discussed in the last chapter, there are a lot of rigging options when it comes to speed jigging. Naturally, Shimano has their own take on this aspect of the game, too. Here's another one of their illustrations, showing the way the Shimano guys do it:

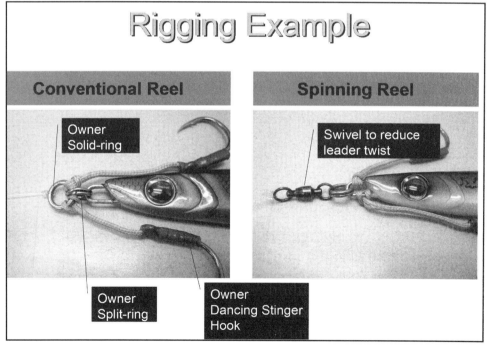

Photo courtesy of Shimano.

Interestingly, despite the fact that this illustration shows twin-hook rigging, I've had Shimano reps tell me the single hook rig is the better way to go, and I've seen other Shimano illustrations that show the Butterfly jigs with single hooks. Again, as stated earlier, there really is no definitive source on this and you'll find reliable sources that give you differing advice on how to rig and fish these jigs.

Since Shimano clearly has a leg up on most tackle outfits when it comes to speed jigging, am I saying everyone should rush right out and buy Shimano gear if they want to apply this tactic? Heck no. Personal preference plays a huge role in finding the "right" fishing tackle for any individual, and you can't simply pick any one brand and say it's "best." What I am hoping to convey, however, is that they did serious research and have already made a lot of the mistakes that many of us would naturally make in trying to put together a jigging package. Emulate the attributes of the Butterfly system, and you'll avoid a lot of hassle.

Shimano rep Justin Poe likes one-hook rigging.... And obviously, it works for him.

Take rods, for example. If you love a fast-action, stiff-tip rod you'll naturally gravitate towards them regardless of the type of fishing you do. But if you get a stiffie for speed-jigging you'll end up wondering why other guys always seem to catch more then you do. (Since your rod tip can't load and unload, and thus your jig's action is greatly reduced.) If you instead get a Trevala, which Shimano designed for this technique, you'll never have to question the rod choice as it applies to Butterfly jigging.

Remember, I am NOT on Shimano's payroll. (Though you Shimano guys should feel free to send me a check any time. Bigger is better.) The fact of the matter is that this company pioneered the development of this specific equipment, and you can benefit from it regardless of the brand you're partial to, budgetary constraints, or any other factors. Okay, enough about Shimano – let's get down to species-specific jigging tactics.

Part II: Species-specific Jigging

Chapter 8: Big Game – Tunas, Wahoo, and Mahi-mahi

Although this chapter focuses on three types of big game fish, it's important to remember that there are differing tactics you'll want to apply for each specific species. There's only one constant, and that's when it comes to tackle — obviously, for these species you'll want to use relatively heavy gear.

My choice for big game jigging is a competent rod & reel, as discussed earlier, spooled with 80-lb. braid. Try using a 100- to 120-pound leader and drop in size as necessary; quite often leader-shy fish like tunas will require going down to 80- or even 60-pound leaders. When it comes to jigs, don't be fooled into believing that bigger is necessarily better — elephants eat peanuts, and it's quite common to catch 100-plus pound fish on the same size jigs you catch five pound bluefish on. Instead, choose jig size according to the depths you need to reach, with deeper fish obviously requiring larger jigs.

Bluefin Tuna

The author tries - unsuccessfully - to hoist a big bluefin up for a photo.

Unlike most tuna species, bluefin can quite often be found in relatively shallow waters. Inshore lumps and structure in waters ranging from 100' to 250' deep are prime territory for these fish, and from North Carolina to New York, that means you can chase big bluefin with runs of 30 miles or less.

The very best situation for jigging bluefin occurs when these fish set up shop over lumps that are inhabited by sand eels. These baits will appear on your meter as green or yellow clouds, on or close to the bottom. Tunas, however, will show up as large red arches. Don't worry about recognizing them for what they are; any decent fishfinder being viewed by any half-experienced angler will make it obvious, as the marks will appear twice as large as those you usually see on-screen. When jigging for bluefin, it's imperative that you locate and spot the fish before you drop and jig. Essentially, you'll want to drop your offering right on top of the fish's head. If you try drifting around and jerking aimlessly, you won't be in for much excitement.

This means you need to go on the hunt: once you're rigged up and ready to rock and roll, be patient and wait for the right moment to drop. If you arrive at an area, hunt around for half an hour, and see a mark or two or some bait on the bottom, there's a lot of temptation to throw the throttles into neutral and give it a shot. Don't. You need to keep on the move until you spot a good cluster of fish that are unquestionably tunas. **This point can not be emphasized enough!** Even if it means putting around in circles half the day before you take a single drop, don't succumb to the temptation to drop on bait marks, or because you "think" there are fish around. Remember — one good drop is all it takes to turn a slow day into the mayhem of a successful tuna hook-up. Hang tough, and keep at it.

What's the best way to proceed with your hunt? When you first arrive at a productive area, stop the boat and allow it to drift while you rig up and get ready. Make sure your chartplotter is set to show your track, and zoomed in as close as possible. Watch that track, to positively ID your drift direction. (You may need to do this several times a day, as wind and current conditions evolve.) Now set up your initial search pattern so you can hunt while going in the exact opposite direction of your drift, at a speed of about six knots. Have your anglers at the ready, on a hair-trigger to drop their jigs the moment you order. This is the prime mode of hunting — spot a fish now, and all you have to do is shift into neutral, turn the boat so the beam is facing the seas, give a yell to the crew, and drop away.

Angler's Tip: *Color preferences of fish will naturally change from place to place and trip to trip, but quite often, pink seems to be a favorite of bluefin tunas found feeding on sand eels.*

Fishing buddy Scott Hyers bagged this bluefin on a pinkie (I know it's in black and white here, but trust me, that jig is pink!) as the trolled and chunked baits from other boats fishing on the Dump Site Lump (out of Indian River, DE) went completely untouched.

Once you've searched as far as you believe to be productive in that direction (you've gone past the edge of the lump or structure, and haven't spotted fish or had a productive drop), you'll have to come about and search in the opposite direction. Many captains will maintain the same speed, then attempt to drop on fish they've passed over — usually to no avail. Stop and drop once you've passed the fish with the current or seas at your stern, and by the time those jigs get down there, you'll usually be well past the fish. Instead, goose the throttles a bit and search at around eight or 10 knots. If you see promising marks don't just shift into neutral, but instead, slow and then come about and see if you can creep back on the fish from the

Captain's Tip

Always remain in forward gear when turning on bluefin, and never shift into reverse and attempt to back up on the fish. There are several reasons for this: first off, many captains (myself included), believe that the clunk of shifting into and out of gear will scare the fish. (Shift into and out of gear with a bluefin on the line and under the boat, if you don't believe me — they'll usually make a nose-diving run for bottom.) Secondly, it's nearly impossible to back up in a straight line for a long enough distance to get back onto fish you went over at eight knots. It's also often unsafe, if you're on a relatively small boat in sizable seas. And finally, on many boats backing will cause turbulence to pass over the fishfinder transducer, either blanking out the screen or creating unreliable readings. If that happens, you won't know when you're over the fish, anyway.

opposite direction, so you're once more going into the sea and/or current, and will drift back onto the fish when you drop.

Okay — so you know how to hunt for the fish, and you've spotted them. What now? When you first locate definite tuna marks, to state the obvious, hit your chartplotter's MOB button so you can return to the spot. Next, take note of the depth the fish are at. If they're dead on bottom drop your jigs until they hit and then give the rod five or six traditional vertical jigging-style sweep-and-drops. Often, this is enough to activate fish and you'll get slammed. Don't worry about setting the hook, because in this scenario the tuna will strike the bait like a freight train. No hits? Then speed jig about half-way to the surface. Often that will activate a strike, but if it doesn't, slide your reel into freespool and drop the jig back down to bottom for another go-round.

Sometimes, you'll spot the fish hanging at mid-depth instead of on bottom. Usually they'll be just below or just above a thermocline; drop until you're confident the jig is a good 20' or 30' below the tunas, and speed jig until your lure comes to the surface. Then immediately freespool, drop the jig back to depth, and start cranking again. If you got the boat over the fish and the jig into the proper position before you started speed jigging, there's a high probability you won't be able to crank it more then once or twice before a bluefin locks its jaws around your lure.

At times yellowfin will also be found on the inshore lumps, and can be targeted with this same hunt-and-drop method. But many seasons,

Sushi, anyone? Fishing Buddy Mike VanCamp says yes.

anglers in search of this species will be forced to fish well offshore. When the yellowfin are hanging deep, the only way to effectively target them is to use a troll-and-drop tactic.

This method is just as simple as it sounds, and has been practiced by a handful of boats (mostly in North Carolina) for several seasons. Here's how it goes: Troll with a fairly small spread which can be quickly cleared; six lines is do-able, but four is better. Have jigging rods rigged and ready, and anglers standing by in the cockpit. When a yellowfin strikes, have your anglers flip jigs into the wash, allow them to drop for 15 to 20 seconds, then speed-jig them back to the boat. If a yellowfin strikes a trolling line and is hooked, leave the hooked rod in the holder and have one or two anglers clear lines while a couple of other anglers toss back jigs. Don't worry about reeling up the hooked fish, because he'll help keep the other tunas swimming close behind your boat. Once another fish or two is hooked up, start cranking on the first one.

Similarly, tossing a jig into the wake of a passing trawler or scalloper will also score at times. Again, allow the jig to drop then jig it a ripping speed jig back to the boat.

This tuna was swimming in the wake of a scalloper, before the girls got their hands on it.

Mahi-Mahi

For some reason, mahi don't seem to be as attracted to metal jigs as other fish. There, I said it. Maybe I just do it wrong, but my logbooks show that serious dolphin anglers will do a heck of a lot better using squid chunks or cast-and-retrieve lures then they will with jigs. So, why even mention them in this context? Because having a jigging rod onboard will help you catch gaffers, instead of chicken.

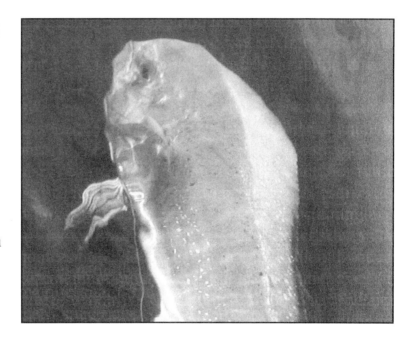

This tactic goes back to the earlier section of this book, where we talked about luring bigger fish up from the depths with a jig by yo-yoing — even though we don't necessarily expect the mahi to take it. So in this case, think of your jig as a fish-attractor, more then as a lure. When you approach an item that you suspect holds mahi, be it a board or a polyball, make sure most of your anglers are armed with traditional mahi-mahi bailing gear: heavy-duty spinning rods rigged with 80-pound leaders terminating in an 8/0 circle hook, baited with fish chunks or whole squid. Toss out your chum chunks, and watch as the two to 10 pounders come rushing in. Watch the crew have a ball bailing them up. But before you move on, drop a jig down at least 150' or so, then speed jig it back up the boat as fast as you possibly can. Every now and again, a 20 to 50 pound gaffer will come charging to the surface, where it will usually slurp down everything in sight — including your angler's baited hooks. Try and offer it the one that's attached to your heaviest bailing rig, and hold on tight.

> **Angler's Tip**
>
> Bait your big mahi-mahi bailing rig with a whole large or horse ballyhoo, hooked through the jaw or eyes. Big dolphin love 'em, but the smaller ones usually can't choke them down so they don't beat the big fish to the punch.

Wahoo

One might expect wahoo to present a similar scenario as dolphin on jigs, but they do not. In fact, they're quite a unique species of fish and present their own challenges and quirks. First, the hooks: the leaders on most standard jigging hooks will hold up for one good wahoo fight, and sometimes two. By the end of the second fight, they're usually frayed and ready for replacement. Unfortunately, quite often when a wahoo strikes it inhales the entire jig, and bites it off cleanly well above the hook. So, even though the hooks can take 'hoo abuse, at least for a fish or two, you'll still have to break out the wire leader if you want a solid shot at catching them. The good news: a trace of six inches is all that's needed to protect your lure.

Thanks to those razor-sharp teeth, you'll want to add a trace of wire above your jig when wahoo are around.

As with mahi, most of the time you'll attack wahoo with jigs is around flotsam. This has nothing to do with where these fish actually are, and has everything to do with our complete inability to find them without a visual hint like a log or a weed paddy. In fact, even with these visual clues it's pretty darn tough to target wahoo with jigs unless they're around in fairly large concentrations. Much of the time if they're present you'll discover them while ripping your jig in, in the hopes of raising a big mahi from the depths—and yes, unlike those big dolphin, a wahoo might just crash that lure. So in this scenario, there's not much to do other then what you would have done already.

There is, however, another measure you can take to generate some wahoo strikes. Again, this takes place while bailing around flotsam. Have a jig rigged with the wire trace, and simply drop it down 70' or 80' below the boat. Adjust the drag to a half-strike setting (to absorb the blow without breaking something — often these fish come on like a ton of bricks) and simply set the rod into a holder. For some reason, the slow, gentle rocking of the boat is often enticing to wahoo that are cruising around below, looking for an easy meal.

Chapter 9: Deepwater Dwellers –Golden Tilefish, Wreckfish, and Grouper

Surprisingly, goldens like this one are suckers for jigs.

Traditional thinkers will tell you that in order to probe the depths at the edge of the continental shelf you'll need broomstick-stout rods, several pounds of lead, and multi-hook rigs. They'll say you need to carry slabs of cut fish, squid, or clams for bait. They'll claim it takes 12 or 15 minutes to reel up your rigs from the 600' to 800' depths you'll be fishing in, and some of these conventional-minded folks will even say an electric reel is a good idea. Hmmm...that doesn't make deep dropping sound like too much fun, does it? Good thing jigs can shed a whole new type of light on deep-dropping.

Grouper will slam jigs, too.

Golden tilefish are likely the deepest species you'll go for, with 650' to 800' being the prime depths. Grouper and wreckfish — very similar species, which we'll consider essentially one and the same for the purposes of this chapter — may also roam this deep, though they can be found as shallow as 400' in the mid-Atlantic region and 100' in southern climes. In waters under 400' regular wreck/reef tactics will apply (see more on this in Chapter 11) but for the purposes of this chapter we'll stick with deepwater fishing, only. In water this deep it'll take a while to hit bottom. Using eight to 14-ounce jigs you can count on several minutes of free-falling. Even using those 750-gram Jerkthatjig whoppers, you'll have to wait a few minutes before touch-down. Diamonds, butterflies, and the like will all do the trick. In the deep water chartreuses and golds with glow-in-the-dark paint seem to work best. No matter what color you choose, make sure you have some glowing going on.

Naturally it's best if there's little wind and current, but you can hold bottom using this gear in a 10 to 15-knot breeze by backing the boat to regain some line now and again. It seems amazing that fish strike jigs without any bait or scent in water this deep, where one would think there's zero light penetration. But they do. Will they eat the bare jigs as often as bait? Not quite: to establish a baseline for jigging effectiveness my boat fished traditional multi-hook deep-drop rigs baited with squid and cut bonito side-by-side with the jigs, on three deep drop excursions. We found that we caught more fish on the baited rigs about three to one over bare jigs.

Meat rigs can be quite effective, as the exceptional fishing buddy David displays.

Here's the kicker: switching to the meat jigging technique completely flip-flopped these numbers, and on one trip, where four lines (two of each type) were deployed at all times, a single jig caught all of the only three goldens of the day. That jig was blue/pink with a glow strip, and the other was a gold/black with a glow strip. Could color patterns possible have an effect in 750' of water? You wouldn't think so, but...

Just as is true in most other forms of jigging, these deep dwelling fish will usually strike the jig as it falls. If it seems to have hit bottom a little too soon, bring the tip of your rod up smartly and set the hook. When you have solid contact, steadily apply pressure. Unlike wreck or reef fishing, there aren't any abrasions or snags for the fish to tangle on, so over-pressuring it to get it away from obstructions isn't necessary.

Without all the added lead, you'll be amazed at how well Mid Atlantic deep-drop fish like golden tilefish will fight. Hook a 40- to 50-pounder — which isn't unusual if you're in the right location — and it'll take you some serious work to bring it up off the bottom. When you've fought the fish about one third of the way, its air bladder will blow and the fish's fighting level will drop noticeably. Pay attention during the fight and try to note when this occurs, because from this point on, that fish is yours. If the hook pulls or your line breaks, the fish's bloated air bladder will float it to the surface. Simply drift for five to 10 minutes, and closely scan the surrounding waters. Sooner or later, you should spot a basketball bobbing around on the surface, within 100' or so of your boat. That's your fish.

When the fish breaks the surface take your time about landing it. Yes, it will often make a desperation run when it sees the boat, but there's no sense in ruining meat with a gaff shot at this point. If the fish thrashes and throws the hook at the surface, it won't be able to dive back down again because of that bloated bladder. You may have to motor after it at time or two as it scuttles away from the boat, but it won't get away. Take your time and insert the gaff hook into the fish's mouth, to bring it aboard.

One exception: if there are a lot of sharks around, you may want to minimize the struggle at the surface for obvious reasons.

The toughest part of deep dropping in the Mid Atlantic is, naturally, figuring out where to do it. Blind drops can result in long, boring drifts without any bites for days at a time. So, how are you going to go from hoping to happening? The first way is to cheat — get a set of numbers from someone who's already located a colony of fish living in the depths. But unless someone owes you big-time, the chances are slim to none that anyone other than a close relative or indentured servant is going share a good set of golden tilefish or snowy grouper numbers with you.

Fortunately, there are a couple of ways you can limit the search area, but in order to do so, we'll have to separate between the two categories of deep dwellers, the tilefish versus the groupers and wreckfish. Why? Because tilefish live on muddy bottoms, where they burrow in and make their own home. There they stay, closely grouped in colonies. Grouper, meanwhile, will be found on hard or rocky bottom — a very different environment.

Fishing buddy Mollie's golden tilefish is excellent eating.

The golden tilefish are a real prize species. These unique fish have a stocky body, a fleshy knob on the head, and a jaw of impressive teeth — keep your fingers clear of 'em. Don't slide a hand into their gills to hold them, either, because their rakers also have teeth that will do a number on you. Most golden tiles weigh between five and 15 pounds, but larger fish are common. Remember that since they live in colonies, most of your catch will often be of similar size. If all you're catching is five-pounders, you're not likely to break the 10-pound mark in the same spot.

Tilefish taste excellent, and their chunky white meat carries the distinct flavor of lobster, one of their favorite foods. Smaller fish may bring less glory, but the lobster flavor is much stronger in them and they generally taste much better then lunkers. Use care when filleting these fish because they have a row of bones along the midsection similar to those found in trout and salmon, running perpendicular to the backbone.

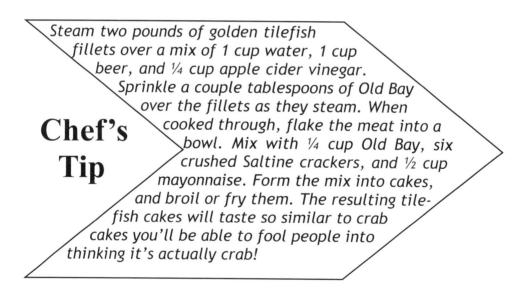

Chef's Tip: Steam two pounds of golden tilefish fillets over a mix of 1 cup water, 1 cup beer, and ¼ cup apple cider vinegar. Sprinkle a couple tablespoons of Old Bay over the fillets as they steam. When cooked through, flake the meat into a bowl. Mix with ¼ cup Old Bay, six crushed Saltine crackers, and ½ cup mayonnaise. Form the mix into cakes, and broil or fry them. The resulting tilefish cakes will taste so similar to crab cakes you'll be able to fool people into thinking it's actually crab!

When you're in tilefish territory, bonus fish in this depth range include black-belly rosefish (orange snapper-like fish in the one-pound range which are excellent eating,) red hake (also small but tasty; note to self — yellowfin tuna will chow these without hesitation when one's live and struggling on the surface) and sharks of all types. If you try tile fishing and catch numerous dog shark, don't blow the remainder of your day in the same spot. When the dog shark migrate along the Continental Shelf they swarm in huge schools, and chances are the tilefish won't ever have a chance to find your baits because the shark will first.

Hake will pop up on your jig when deep dropping, too.

To go scouting for golden tilefish, first identify plateaus in 650' to 850' of water right along the edge of the shelf. Then, prospect the area with a home-made bottom sampler. Attach a 6" piece of copper or lead pipe to a sash weight, drop it on a line, and drag it across the bottom. If you discover sand, silt, or grey mud, eliminate the area from consideration. If you locate the firm green mud tilefish prefer, however, the spot could be a winner. Fish the area until you hook a single fish, and immediately note your position. Mark it on the GPS, pull up-wind, and do another drift on a parallel track about an eighth of a mile away from the original one. Again, plot any bites. Now do a third drift an eighth of a mile off in the other direction from the original drift. Eventually, you'll be able to identify where the fish are clustered. This is a lot more important than many people think, especially when it comes to golden tilefish, because their colonies are tightly packed together. In fact, 80-percent of the fish in a colony will be within 100' to 200' of each other — a tiny target in a very, very big ocean.

The good news: once you locate a colony, it doesn't go anywhere. You can return to the spot over and over again, so long as you don't fish it out. Of course, this is a distinct possibility with golden tilefish, which are very slow growers. Smart anglers will limit themselves to 30 or 40 pounds of fish or, in the case of large tilefish, a single fish per person. That's plenty of meat, and from 800' below, plenty of cranking for one day.

The bad news: since these are such slow growers, it's all too easy to fish a spot out. In fact, one of the best spots I've ever found went dry within three years, even though no more then a half-dozen boats had the set of numbers.

Hunting for new grouper and wreckfish spots in the deep is a bit easier, because a high-quality fishfinder will tell you the entire story. All you need to do is keep half an eye on the fishfinder all day, as you troll for other offshore species. Just zoom it up on the bottom, and look for bottom lines that suddenly become extremely thin. Remember: bottom type is indicated on-screen in a form that's counter-intuitive. Thick bottom readings indicate soft or sandy bottoms (which are absorbing some of the signal, before bouncing it back) while hard rocky bottoms will appear as very thin bottom lines.

Wreckfish will be found on hard bottom or wrecks, as opposed to mud bottom.

Save waypoints as you spot promising areas, and come back to them later when you're ready to focus solely on jigging.

Once you have a bunch of potential hard spots to try, you can hop from one to the next, dropping jigs at each, until you get lucky. And with a heavy jig on the end of a braid mainline,

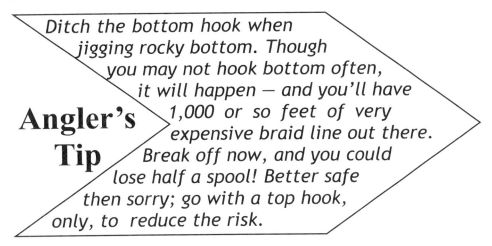

Angler's Tip: Ditch the bottom hook when jigging rocky bottom. Though you may not hook bottom often, it will happen — and you'll have 1,000 or so feet of very expensive braid line out there. Break off now, and you could lose half a spool! Better safe then sorry; go with a top hook, only, to reduce the risk.

you'll be able to feel the metal pinging off rocks, when you're in the right type of bottom structure areas.

Note that whatever type of bottom you're dropping over, staying in touch with it is imperative. The fish discussed in this chapter all live within a few feet of bottom and if your jig gets pulled up by the current, you won't get bit. After making initial contact with the bottom you should be re-dropping every few times you jig, to ensure that your lure is still all the way down there. When there's a stiff breeze or a strong current, you may need to drop back additional line every 10 or 15 seconds. If it seems nearly impossible to keep that jig down there, crank it back in and trade up for a heavier jig.

Of course, one of the most interesting aspects of deep-dropping is that you never know exactly what will end up on the line. Conger eels, anglerfish, hagfish — anything is possible, when you're probing the depths at the Continental Shelf.

Chapter 10: Other Bottom Fish – Blueline Tilefish, Rosies, and Shark

In shallower (300' to 600') water just inside the edge of the Continental shelf you'll encounter blueline tilefish, but none of the big golden tilefish. Bluelines are similar in body shape to

Blueline tilefish have the golden's body but very different coloration, as fishing buddy Boomer shows

goldens but their uniform blue coloration is very different. They also don't grow nearly as big, with a 10-pounder being a real whopper. Their meat is darker and oilier then golden tiles, but its taste is excellent. In this depth range you'll also hook a wide range of other species, including such fish as rosies, four-spot flounder, hake, sharks, and black sea bass. (We'll cover black sea bass in depth in Chapter 11, since they're more commonly targeted over wrecks then open bottom.)

Jigging in this zone is a bit easier, as your jig will hit bottom faster and will stay there with a bit less work. A dozen or so ounces will do the trick quite often, and you rarely need to resort to those three-pound monster jigs. If strong wind and current does force you to opt for monster jigs, however, don't worry they'll out-size the fish. Bluelines of five or more pounds (somehow!) have no problem inhaling a foot-long jig, and it seems to be impossible to use jigs that are too big to get eaten.

Again, as when jigging for golden tilefish, grouper, and wreckfish, meat-jigging is often more effective then swinging a bare jig with the traditional vertical-jigging style. Blueline tiles in particular will show a clear preference for a jig with a chunk of smelly fish or squid

Blueline tilefish have huge mouths for their size, and they aren't afraid of extremely large jigs.

dangling off the hook. Same goes regarding bait for rosies, although in their case, a two-pounder is a whopper. Still, their mouths are huge and they don't hesitate when trying to eat a jig literally as large as they are. For deepwater sea bass, however,

Rosies (properly called black-belly rose fish) are a common accidental catch.

jigging without the meat will generate the most strikes. In fact, sea bass rarely need the added temptation of bait when you find these fish in the deep because they're often relatively big (four pounds

As fishing buddy Jack discovered when this fish took a vertically-jigged spoon, sea bass will hit in surprisingly deep waters.

or more) and very, very aggressive. Treat them accordingly. Quickly-jigged spoons presented vertically and/or speed-jigged within 20' or 30' of the bottom, then re-dropped, usually tempts sea bass beyond their ability to resist. If you have numbers for wreck in these middle of the road, 300' to 600' depths, they're almost sure to hold big bass. Of course, anchoring this deep can be quite problematic, so drifting over the wreck is usually the tactic you'll need to apply. And remember: when drifting over a wreck, stick with single top-hook rigging, and you'll experience a fraction of the snags and break-offs usually associated with drifting over a wreck.

It's difficult to specify the best bottom type for mid-depth bottom fish like bluelines, four-spots, and open-water bass, and how to find it, mostly because experience has proven they'll show up clustered over varying bottom types. Many anglers claim you need hard bottom, and of course, being over a wreck or similarly dramatic structure never hurts when it comes to finding fish like sea bass. But the bluelines live over soft bottom and from what I've seen these fish may pop up anywhere near the edge of the shelf, close to the big drop-off. Using your fishfinder zoomed in on bottom is, again, the key to locating them. Most of the time these fish are visible on-screen. Or, at least, the bait they are feeding on is visible; truth be told I don't know exactly what I'm looking at, but marks can be seen when over a patch of bluelines and bass over open bottom. These aren't usually the big red arches we're used to identifying as large gamefish. Rather, some snow-like markings appear on-screen within five or 10' of the bottom, with dots that look notably larger then clutter. Occasionally, you'll see a larger mark or two mixed in. When you see this "heavy" snow, give it a shot.

One interesting thing you'll notice about good blueline/bass spots in the 300' to 400' range: often when lobster gear is set in these depths, you'll see their orange polyball floats all over the

Captain's Tip

The presence of those polyballs where you find bluelines makes for a natural game plan: Deep drop for tilefish, then bail for mahi-mahi. Remember, those polyballs provide cover for mahi and these fish can often be found hovering just below them.

place – the lobster and the bluelines must like the same conditions. When you see these polyballs (you'll also see them in deeper water when targeting golden tilefish) don't forget that they have a huge "trawl" under each float, with dozens of pots attached to a single line. You may think you're safe from snagging that lobster pot line while fishing a half mile away from the nearest float, but you're not. And if you snag bottom in one of these soft-bottom areas, remember: there's not much to snag down there. Chances are you've got one of those lobster pot lines, and if you keep making the same drift you'll snag it again and again. With

When you see polyballs in the area, be sure to bail them. Fishing buddy JP did, and found it well worthwhile.

hundreds of yards of braid in the water, this can become a pretty expensive problem so you might want to alter locations.

Shark are, of course, not commonly targeted by jiggers. But there's one species which will commonly hit jigs, and which you will almost certainly encounter if you spend a fair amount of time jigging on bottom in these depths: Atlantic sharpnose. These sharks are easily identifiable by the white splotches along their sides. The run from three to five feet, and are commonly 10 to 25 pounds. Unlike many sharks these are edible. Truth be told, however, I haven't found them to be excellent table fare. So when you catch that shark with splotches along its flanks you may want to take one home to try out, but releasing them would be an even better idea.

Atlantic sharpnose strike jigs a lot more often then one would imagine; they're easily identified thanks to the white splotches on their flanks.

Chapter 11: The Wrecking Crew – Sea Bass, Snappers, and Grouper

Wreck fishing can be a ton of fun – non-stop action, a wide variety of species, and good table fare is all part of this game. In northern and Mid Atlantic waters sea bass, tautog, and flounder are the main species, and as you hit Virginia and North Carolina waters, snappers and grouper can be added to the list. Occasionally open-water species like king mackerel, mahi-mahi and tunas will make a showing around wrecks. If you're dropping bottom rigs baited with squid or cut fish, the usual method

Sea bass are the number one target, for most wreck anglers in the Mid Atlantic.

of targeting wreck-dwellers, these pelagics will come and go without you ever knowing; jiggers, however, will get to experience the shock and thrill of the unexpected.

Surprise! As Fishing buddies Brian & Chris have seen, you just never know what's going to strike a jig while wreck fishing. On one trip, that included king mackerel.

Wrecks are best approached with an amalgamation of jigging techniques. You'll find that vertical jigging right over the wreck will be most effective when the fish are holding close to the structure. When sea bass are suspended above it, however, they seem completely unable to resist the strike-generating action of speed jigging. Those targeting grouper will find that meat jigging also proves most effective at times.

Vertical jigging is the easiest and fastest way to load the box (when the fish appreciate it, of course,) since the lure remains in the strike zone at all times and requires no baiting, so savvy anglers will start with this method and change up as necessary.

Jig size should be judged according to the depth of the wreck, and you should generally use the lightest possible while maintaining the ability to get down fast, and stay there. Don't worry about out-sizing the fish; again, you'll find that sea bass are ambitious fish and will strike jigs as large as they are.

Another advantage jiggers gain over bait fishermen: your average fish will be notably larger. While small sea bass will eat large jigs, the beasts ruling the roost are often the ones to attack a moving jig first. But, there's one disadvantage, too: if it's possible to catch a tog on a jig, I haven't seen it happen yet. So jiggers will give up their shot at that one species.

Wreck fishing is certainly one scenario in which you'll want to drop jigs with a single top hook, only. These rarely get snagged in the wreckage, while traditional treble hook jigs with the treble placed on the tail will get snagged time and time again. Even with the single top hook, however, you will occasionally get snagged. To prevent the loss of large amounts of expensive braid line, wreck jiggers should spool up with relatively light leaders. Thirty pound test wind-ons are appropriate, and as long as your mainline is 60 pound test or more, you can go to 40 or 50 pound leaders. However you rig up just make sure that the leader will break before the main line, so you don't have a break-off with lots of line out and end up ruining your entire spool.

Whenever the topic of wreck fishing comes up, the drift vs. anchor debate invariably comes up. So which is better, drifting or anchoring? Neither and both. Anchoring allows you to sit dead over the wreck — if you hit it right, which can mean anchoring and re-anchoring several times to get into the best position. But it also means you're stuck in one location, and if it's a poor one or if you hit it hard for several hours and stop catching fish, you have to start all over again from ground zero. Drifting, on the other hand, allows you to maintain your flexibility. If one side of a wreck isn't producing you can simply shift over to the other side. Each time you drift along the wreck you're exposing your jig to new territory with potentially more and bigger fish, and you're also exposing it to more wreckage, dragging along it and thus boosting the chance of snags. Plus, minus, plus, minus — pick your poison. That said, personally I tend to drift far more often then anchoring, simply because it allows me to move on quickly when I don't like the results. Plus, it gives me hope that at any second, my jig might drift past the jaws of a big, hungry fish that wouldn't have otherwise seen my offering. Hope springs eternal.

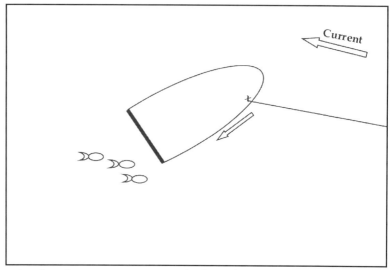

Anchoring may mean missing the target; if you're close enough, however, you may be able to "swing" the boat over the wreck (and the fish) by attaching the line to a spring cleat.

Captain's Tip

When wreck fishing pay particularly close attention to the current. As it changes the fish will commonly shift position on the wreckage, and a hotspot can go cold in minutes. When the bite stops don't assume the fish have quit - try a different section of wreckage. Sometimes, just slacking back 50' or 60' of anchor line or "swinging" on a spring cleat is all it takes to completely change the bite.

> **Angler's Tip**
>
> *Regardless of whether you're vertical jigging or speed jigging, more and faster motion is almost always best when targeting wreck fish. Though it may sound strange, these fish really like to attack a bait that's trying to flee. You may note that both bass and grouper share similar body, tail, and jaw shapes, because both are ambush predators that rush in with a sudden burst of speed to suck in their prey. That fast jigging action is often what triggers the burst of speed.*

When you want to specifically target sea bass on wrecks, you'll want to locate the fish on your meter and judge depth accordingly. Bass often hold right on the wreck but commonly will also suspend 10', 20', or even 30' above it. Grouper, however, are almost always found holding very, very tight to the structure. You'll have to keep your offering up close and personal to the wreck, and remember that when a grouper strikes, it'll do its best to go right back into that wreckage. Hit it with maximum drag right from the start, and don't let up one bit until you have the fish a good 20' to 30' off the wreck. Often, shortly after getting them clear the fish will turn their head down and run like a bull for the bottom. Again, hold 'em. This is the make or break moment, and although over-pressuring the fish may lead to the "break" part of that saying, if you allow the fish to get back to the structure there's a very good chance it'll tangle your line or pull it against something sharp.

Depth is another factor you'll want to keep in mind when targeting sea bass versus grouper. Bass can be found in wrecks as shallow as 40' or 50', while grouper are rarely found (keeper sized, anyway) in wrecks anywhere near that shallow. Mostly, this is a function of convenience; wrecks that are close to shore are hit hard and often and quickly become fished out, while deeper, farther wrecks are not.

It's hard to pinpoint a specific depth to start searching for grouper in earnest, because to some degree, it depends on geography. Generally speaking, the farther south you go the shallower you can find them. Go on a search for grouper out of Virginia, for example, and you're not likely to find success until you're probing in 400' or more of water. Off the coast of North Carolina, however, you will commonly catch plenty of grouper in 70' or 80' of water (though most will be throw-backs, again, a function of keeper fish being fished out).

Keeper-sized grouper like this gag held by fishing buddy Brother Robert will usually come from relatively deep waters.

Sea bass, on the other hand, will be found in both the shallower and deeper waters. It is still true, however, that larger fish are much more common the deeper you go — few anglers run 40 or 50 miles to 200'-plus deep wrecks to target bass. If you want to enjoy stellar bass fishing, that's exactly what you should do.

Here's some weird sea bass trivia: most fish are hermaphrodites, and reproduce as both male and female at different points in time. They start out as females when they first mature, and by the time they hit six years of age on average, their ovaries become non-functional and they begin creating sperm. An even weirder fact: in areas where the bass are heavily fished, they may begin to change sex at an earlier age in response to the lack of males.

Snapper are only available to southern anglers, mostly from the Carolinas south. As a result I haven't spent a heck of a lot of time targeting them and I certainly can't claim to be any expert on them, but on regular forays south there is one thing I've learned about snapper on wrecks and reef bottom: they love to smack vertically jigged lures. Red snapper, white grunt, yellow "bank" sea bass, speckled hind, and numerous other reef dwellers regularly smack jigs intended for groupers and sea bass.

Kingfish will also attack jigs near wrecks and reefs, though to catch these fish you'll have to be quick on the draw. Usually it happens when a school of kings goes zipping over or around a wreck, and you're retrieving a jig in speed jigging fashion. Several times it's happened on my boat purely by accident — someone was reeling in and got

Snapper like the one caught by fishing buddy Jason will be encountered on southern wrecks and reefs, too.

lucky. But that doesn't mean you can't target these fish in specific with jigs. The key here is to find what the fish are sticking close to: bait. When you see a cloud of baitfish moving at mid-depth on the meter, dropped jigs just below them and speed jigged back through the fish. If kings are around, they'll spot those jigs and move in for the kill.

You'll also catch your fair share of those Atlantic Sharpnose sharks when vertical jigging around wrecks. Though it may seem a bit strange, jigs worked vigorously will often catch the attention of these sharks, and as we mentioned earlier, they'll strike metal without hesitation. (When speed jigging, however, they generally leave you alone.)

Though they're not incredibly impressive sharks note that they have a set of small but sharp teeth, and can put a hurting on you if you aren't careful when un-hooking your jig. Unlike many sharks Atlantic sharpnose are edible, though as discussed in the prior chapter their meat isn't incredibly flavorful.

Chapter 12: Inshore Gamefish – Stripers, Blues, Amberjack, Fluke, and Weakfish

Fishing for each of these species is incredibly different. As you probably already know, stripers and weakfish, as an example, play very different parts in the ecosystem. So it's impossible to generalize about each of these species; instead, we'll address them one by one.

Stripers

Stripers are one of the most popular gamefish in existence.

Striped bass AKA stripers AKA rockfish AKA damn good eating are one of the most popular sportfish in existence, and appear in good numbers along the coast and in coastal bays at different times depending on your geographic location and the season. New Yorkers and Jersey anglers will have them in town during the warm months, Mid Atlantic anglers will get into stripers almost year-round in the Chesapeake region and in incredible numbers along the coast (particularly at the CBBT) early in the winter, and Carolina anglers get in on the action later in the winter (if it gets cold enough) most years. Regardless of where you happen to be when the stripers roll through, one thing is for sure: you can catch them by jigging.

 I hate to be the bearer of bad news, but I've got to say, modern speed jigging techniques really don't work well with stripers. I've yet to hit 'em hard speed jigging, and I have yet to talk to one single person who has. Why? My best guess is that it's because stripers are basically lazy fish. They're usually looking for easy pickin's, and chasing after a baitfish that's zooming away doesn't count as easy. That said, this doesn't mean other forms of jigging aren't a killer. In fact, jigging is my favorite way to target striped bass.

 Which form of jigging will work best depends heavily on the situation. When stripers are stacked up and are visible either via working birds or on the fishfinder, vertical jigging with metal or plastics rigged on leadheads is the way to go. Stripers will go ballistic on the standard vertical jigging technique when they're suspended, and all you have to do is identify the key depth and put your lure there. Fast or slow vertical jigging may be in order depending on the mood of the fish, and in waters less then 30' or so it's usually a good idea to get your jig away from the boat a bit. In water this depth or less stripers may shy away from the boat, especially if you have a rumbly two-stroke outboard. In any case, when they're shallow and particularly when they're feeding at or near bottom, flipping a Fin-S or twister style jig tail on a leadhead away from the boat then jigging it as you retrieve along bottom, is often a killer technique. Every few hops let the jig sink until you feel contact with the bottom to be sure you're moving slowly enough, and when there's a fast drift (and a large angle on your line when you let it out,) you may be able to simply let out line until the lure hits bottom and jig it without retrieving as you move along.

As usual, color preferences will be dictated by the shade of the water. Generally speaking, as usual matching your lure color to the color of the water is the most effective way to go. In the murky green Chesapeake waters try chartreuse, in inshore ocean waters go for lime green, and in clearer northern waters blue is often a good bet. Pink will also rock at times and plain silver is always a safe bet.

Size-wise, picking the best jig is a matter of matching the hatch. When stripers are feeding on bay anchovies or similarly small baitfish, drop your spoon down as small as you can stand it. If they're preying on larger bunker, however, up-size the spoon to match it. You'll also find these fish feeding on sand eels along inshore shoals off the coast at times, particularly during the fall migration run going down the coats. In this situation, choose a spoon with a long, thin profile. Almost without fail, vertical jigging right on bottom will prove the most successful method when sand eels are on the menu.

When stripers are feeding at or near bottom, hopping a plastic jig along the bottom is a top tactic — one which fishing buddy Instant Jeff applied successfully.

Angler's Tip

When stripers are breaking water, nine times out of 10 the smallest fish in the school are the ones churning the surface. Remember, stripers are essentially lazy fish that will take an easy meal over one they have to work for, any day of the year. Larger stripers will hang below the pack, picking off injured fish at their leisure. To target the big boys, go with heavy jigging spoons like Butterflies, Hopkins, Stingsilvers, and Williamsons, drop them down deep below the main school, and vertically jig to catch 'em up.

Stripers holding deep over drop-offs, channel edges, and similar forms of structure call for a different jigging technique. Yes, you'll get some by vertically jigging, but in this situation you'll catch more fish by presenting a bait that appears to be moving horizontally through the water column. To target stripers in this situation, try dropping down prior to driving over the fish as you idle along. Make sure you do so early enough that you have contact with the bottom before passing over the fish, and pull your boat out of gear when you see the school thick on the meter. Jig your rod with slow sweeps towards the bow of the boat, and drop back slowly enough to maintain tension at all times. Then shift your boat into and out of gear as necessary to keep the boat moving forward, but slowly enough that you maintain contact with the bottom every time you drop back your rod tip. Think of this tactic somewhat like traditional bottom-bouncing; you want the jig to stay near bottom at all times — and may well need to let out additional line as you go down sharp edges or into channels — but you don't want to allow the jig to drag or sit on bottom.

When targeting stripers with this tactic, make sure you rig a treble hook on the aft end of the jig. You'll get a LOT of short strikes otherwise, probably because stripers holding deep in this situation usually aren't feeding very aggressively. The horizontally-traveling jig will trigger a reaction strike but it's often a pretty half-hearted one, so make sure that treble's there to grab onto 'em. You can also use plastics to apply this tactic, though only in relatively shallow water. Even with a whopping two-ounce jig head, it's tough to get plastics to stay close to the bottom when water depth is much over 30' and the boat's moving at all.

What about stripers holding tight to inlet rocks? Fish cruising the surf? Migrating stripers on the move? Those holding in rips? In these and most other situations you might catch a fish or two by jigging, but you'll catch more with other techniques: bait, surface plugs, cast and retrieved plastics, etc.

Bluefish

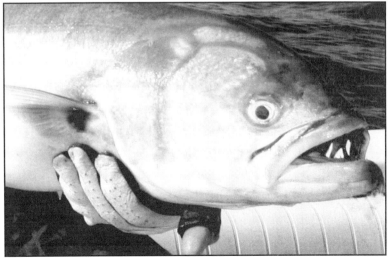

Watch those teeth!

Bluefish are the bane of some anglers, and the love of others. They fight hard, bite with abandon, and taste... well, you know. Jigging isn't normally the preferred method of targeting blues, simply because bait is so darn effective with these fish. If it has scales and it smells like fish, a blue will eat it without hesitation. But jigging still has its place, when it comes to blues. Speed jigging, that is. Try vertical jigging and every second or third fish your line will go slack, and stay that way. You never felt even a hint of tension? That just goes to show you how sharp a blue's teeth are — they can cut both mono and braid, without an iota of tension on the line.

You could add wire to your leader but speed jigging works for these fish simply because they almost always get metal, instead of mono, in their mouth. Unless, that is, they strike as your jig falls... in which case you're out $10 or $15. Most of the time, though speed-jigged blues find the hook instead of the leader. That said, even the heavy hook leader fibers used for jigging hooks will get worn out by bluefish. Every fourth or fifth fish, check that leader closely and make sure he hasn't worn it away.

> **Angler's Tip**
> When blues are breaking water prevent bite-offs on a falling jig by casting well beyond the fish, before you begin your retrieve.

So, when and how should you jig for blues? Any time you know they're in the area, either by seeing them on the surface of having caught them on the troll, start speed jigging. If the fish are there, they'll see the jigs and smash 'em. If you want to specifically target blues on jigs, however, then drop anchor in a likely area and set up a chum line. Ground menhaden works best, and it doesn't take much — put a frozen block of chum over the side and bluefish will come slashing their way to the boat, sometimes to strike the chum block itself. Put a bait or two in the slick so you see the strikes and know when to get busy, then cast a metal jig as far back as possible and zing it through the slick at top speed. Warning: do not try this with a soft plastic! Do so, and you'll reel in half a lure, time and time again.

Bluefish are incredibly plentiful all up and down the coast, and locating these fish when they're in season usually isn't too tough. Any shoal, structure, or channel edge is likely to hold them, any time and place the water temperature ranges from the mid 60's to the upper 70's. You'll also spot them quite often in open water, making mincemeat out of pods of baitfish.

Amberjack

Jacks aren't much good as a food fish, but they do bite willingly then pull like a mule — hence the nickname "wreck donkey" — so many anglers give them a high rating as a gamefish. They'll be found from Maryland south most seasons, usually hanging above a wreck, around the legs of markers, and near other significant forms of structure. Unlike many other fish they are often found well off of the structure, and seem to like to hold halfway from the structure to the surface when found over wrecks.

When amberjack are located on the meter you can drop a lure down to them and vertically jig it. But the fact that they suspend makes amberjacks prime candidates for speed jigging, and they just so happen to react positively to a chunk of metal zinging by at a high rate of speed.

As when speed jigging for suspended tunas, you'll want to drop your jig well past the depth the fish are holding at, then speed jig it all the way up to the surface. As soon as it comes up close to the boat, if it hasn't been hit simply re-drop it and start over again. Beyond that there isn't too terribly much to talk about; if these fish are present and a jig goes flying past at a high rate of speed, you're almost certainly going to experience the tugging of a wreck donkey. Note: remember that these fish are considered poor food-fish, before you sink a gaff or box an amberjack.

Fluke

Fluke AKA flounder AKA flatties is another type of fish that reacts far better to jigging then most anglers know. In fact, once you discover how effective jigging for these fish is, I'll bet you leave the minnow bucket and squid at home on future fluking trips.

There's one difference between jigging for flounder and jigging for many other inshore sportfish which should be painfully obvious: you want to keep that jig dead on bottom, at all times, period. Your up-swing should take your jig no more then three

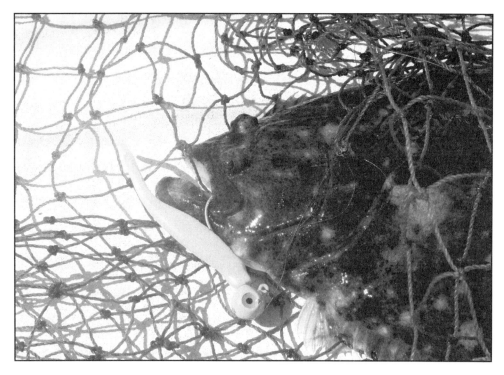

Leave the minnow bucket and squid at home, because flounder are suckers for vertically-jigged soft plastics.

feet, and you should always, always feel it touch bottom on the down-swing. Unless, of course, a flounder slams your jig before it can sink all the way.

Naturally, this fact eliminates speed-jigging, yo-yoing, and most other methods except for vertical jigging. Otherwise, most of the usual jigging truths hold fast: the fish may prefer a fast jig on day one and a slow one the next; they may like a short lift or a long one, etcetera.

Plastic body twister or paddle tail jigs in the four-inch range are a great flounder lure that will be eaten by these other fish any day of the week. Chartreuse is a top color choice, but white seems to hold a slight edge some days. In off-colored water yellow is often the ticket, and in low-light conditions, purple sometimes out-catches all other choices. A bucktail dressed with a chunk of peeler crab, a squid strip, or a fat bull minnow is also a good lure to jig with. For some reason, heavy metal and resin spoons do not seem to work incredibly well on this species of fish.

As usual the vast majority of your hits will come as the jig sinks, and often you can detect a hit simply by noting that your lure seems to hit bottom a few feet before you expected it to. Unlike bait fishing for fluke, when they chew on the bait before taking it completely into their mouths and you'll miss the fish if you set the hook at the first sign of a bite, flounder will usually inhale a jig all the way on their initial attack. Accordingly, as soon as you detect a strike set the hook with gusto.

There are a few other tactical changes you'll want to make when jigging for flounder, in specific. In offshore waters (you'd be amazed at how deep you can catch flounder — we've caught "four spot" flounder in water as deep as 600') most of the flatfish you catch will be located around the edges of wrecks and reefs. Unlike sea bass, grouper, or other wreck dwellers, the fluke are nearly always off to the sides. That makes drifting mandatory; anchor up over the wreck, and your chance of catching flounder goes down dramatically. Inshore you'll find them just as often on shoals and edges, as on the wrecks or reefs. Finally, remember that flounder are sight-feeders. Bright, sunny days and calm, clear water is usually the best time to fish for them. When the water is discolored and heavy cloud cover is overhead, you're usually better served by targeting other species.

Bright, sunny days are the best for flounder jigging.

Sea Trout & Weakfish

Weakfish, also known as sea trout or yellowfin sea trout, are total suckers for vertical jigging. Their close relative, the speckled sea trout, is usually lured to the hook by a horizontally-moving jig, especially since they're usually found in water too shallow for a vertical presentation. So even though these fish are closely related, we'll have to separate them a bit, when discussing tactics.

This hefty spec slammed a soft plastic hopped along the bottom.

Weakfish are unlike all other fish you'll ever jig for, because sometimes the best presentation to get 'em to bite is to simply drop a jig to depth, stick your rod in a holder, and ignore it. "Dead-sticking," as it's known on the Chesapeake Bay, is the best way to generate sea trout bites about 10 or 20 percent of the time. That may not sound like a lot, but compare it to other species, which like this presentation somewhere between zero percent of the time and never.

When does dead-sticking work? I don't have a good answer; logs and experience have not proven any specific pattern with regards to current, light levels, depth, or any other obvious factor. All I can tell you is sometimes it works; if you know weakies are in the area and you can't buy a bite, try it.

Otherwise, most of the time vertical jigging with metal or resin spoons is the way to go. Both slack drops and tensioned drops can be effective, and like many predators, weakfish almost always strike jigs as they're falling. Blue, pink, and chartreuse seem to be their favorite colors, in that order, for once regardless of water color. Speed jigging will trigger strikes, but since weakies usually hold near the bottom, in most cases speed jigging merely pulls the jig quickly out of their target zone. On top of that, these fish are called weakfish because their jaws are so flimsy, and hooks rip out of them depressingly easily. Speed jig, and you'll often pull in a chunk of the weakfish's mouth with no weakfish attached. So remember: when it comes to weakfish, think vertical.

Weakfish will often be located in deepwater channels where they've set up shop for an extended period of time. Unlike many other inshore gamefish they'll sit very deep, sometimes as deep as 100'. Nine times out 10 they'll be hugging bottom, and appear on the fishfinder as a long red caterpillar, hovering a foot or two above the bottom reading. Sometimes trout will sit in holes or channels for months at a time, providing a reliable target to jiggers for an extended period. The same goes for inlet mouths, where they'll also set up shop. Inlets with deep holes at the ends, scoured out of the sand by countless rushing tides, are prime territory.

As trout migrate up or down the coast you'll also locate them over shoals in the 20' to 40' range. Usually these are fish on the move, though, and may be here today and gone tomorrow. Commonly, you'll get a shot at them for a couple of weeks before they move on.

In many areas of the Mid Atlantic region, weakfish have been in short supply for the past few years. Their populations hit a high in the late 90's, then slowly dropped, and by 2002 or 2003 they became down-right scarce in many areas.

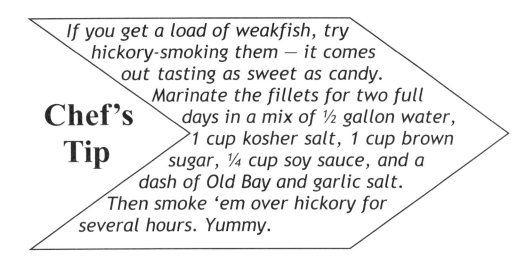

Chef's Tip: If you get a load of weakfish, try hickory-smoking them — it comes out tasting as sweet as candy. Marinate the fillets for two full days in a mix of ½ gallon water, 1 cup kosher salt, 1 cup brown sugar, ¼ cup soy sauce, and a dash of Old Bay and garlic salt. Then smoke 'em over hickory for several hours. Yummy.

Though this caps off the list of fish we'll examine in specific, remember that you can catch just about anything, utilizing these different forms of jigging. Oddball catches through the years includes barracuda, lizard fish, live squid, toad fish, rudder fish — you name it, it might just grab your jig.

What is it that makes jigging so exciting — is it the ability to use light gear on powerhouse fish? The idea of catching fish on lures, from hundreds of feet below? The fact that this technique is, in many situations, the most effective way to get your rod bent over under the pressure of a pelagic predator? Whatever aspect of jigging gets you fired up, I hope you've discovered some new and interesting techniques in *Rudow's Guide to Modern Jigging*. Even sitting here at the keyboard I can feel the anticipation of the swing, drop, and swing. Crank, lift, crank. Jerk, jerk, jerk. That bone-shattering hit will come any second, now... any second. I hope you feel that same anticipation, and I hope that you'll find this book useful and helpful, as you set out to catch more, bigger fish. As to the fishing buddies who haven't been pictured in this book: I chose pictures according to who was holding the fish, so obviously, you just need to come out fishing with me more often!

As always, I'll be happy to answer any specific questions readers may have after looking through this book. You can always reach me via the "Ask An Expert" section on www.HookedOnFishingBoats.com. (Where you can also visit my blog.) And, you can find fishing gear reviews, how-to fishing articles, and gobs of other fishing-oriented info on my web site www.FishingGearGuru.com. Thanks, and good luck getting jiggly with it!

Your fishing buddy,
Lenny Rudow

Check out these other how-to/where-to fishing books, by Lenny Rudow.

The **Rockfish Guide** digs deep into striped bass, why they act the way they do, and how to target them with dozens of specific tactics. **Fishing the Mid Atlantic** details over 300 hotspots along the coast from North Carolina to New York, including bay, inlet, and ocean hotspots (including GPS coordinates for wrecks, canyons, and more.) The **Chesapeake Guide** is the classic how-to/where-to fishing bible of the Chesapeake Bay.

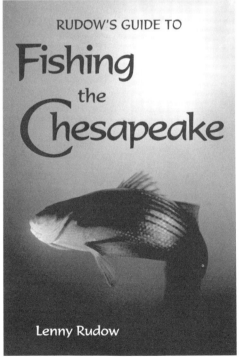

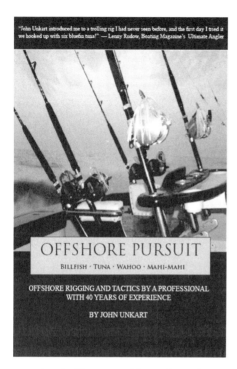

And these other hard-core how-to/where-to fishing books, written by pros for serious anglers. All are available at:

www.schifferbooks.com